"We do not need miracles t[...]
we only need ea[...]

Shaherazad Un[...]

The travels within this book were completed with the support of The Winston Churchill Memorial Trust and The Rank Foundation, through the awarding of a Winston Churchill Memorial Trust Fellowship for Enterprise. The core purpose of the Churchill Fellowship and consequently Each Other is to provide a practical toolkit of best practice to enable women to empower women within the United Kingdom in particular. The findings are intended to help females to make the world a gender equal and happy place; for now and for future generations. Some of the travels which took place prior to 2018 were partially funded by the Department for International Trade (United Kingdom).

The Rank Foundation
Winston Churchill Memorial Trust
Department for International Trade

The Winston Churchill Memorial Trust runs the Churchill Fellowships, a unique programme of overseas research grants. These support UK citizens from all parts of society to travel the world in search of innovative solutions for today's most pressing problems. Every year they fund outstanding individuals to travel anywhere in the world, researching a topic of their choice among global leaders in their field. At the heart of all this is a simple but enduring concept. The Trust is empowering individuals to learn from the world, for the benefit of the UK. Today this idea is more valuable than ever.

The Rank Foundation aims to improve the lives of people and their communities across the United Kingdom. This is done through encouraging enterprise and innovation. It has jointly funded the research grant for Enterprise with The Winston Churchill Memorial Trust.

Each Other is a dissemination of the learning on women's empowerment by Shaherazad Umbreen.

The Department for International Trade secures UK and global prosperity by promoting and financing international trade and investment, and championing free trade.

For Women The World Over

Each Other

Why Women Must Empower Women

Contents

Hear From: Farah Alali

Burkas, Burkinis and Bikinis
For Each Other: Toolkit Actions 20, 21

Food For Female Thought
For Each Other: Toolkit Action 22
Hear From: Laurine
Hear From: Sheyla
Hear From: In'am

For Each Other: The Collection of Toolkit Actions

Think and take action to unite
Foster the courage to speak out
Champion relatable and unrelatable women
Understand gender challenges
Everyday activism
Provide platforms where women can learn
Look, look and look again
Have the audacity to educate
Spot the men of average talent
Remember that giving birth isn't easy
Get social
Take a chance
Hold to account
Disband the Man Club
Mind your language
Mind their language

Positive discrimination can have a positive place
Encouraging women to infantilise men has got to stop
Equality education must start in school and remain on
the agenda in all workplaces
Sexual misdemeanours are never ever okay
Notice and call out gendered ruthlessness
Feed the world, including all of the women
Take part in collective action … with heart

Hear From: Helen Pankhurst

Part 14: Conclusion   264

Each Other

Part 15: End Notes   266

Post Script: My Wish for our World
Gender Glossary
References
Appendix
Further Reading
Start Empowering Today
Acknowledgements
The Author

Why This Book Exists

Part 1

A Bold Assertion

It was the day I realised why.

Why there is not a single country in the world where women have full equality with men. Not one. Why more girls than boys experience extreme hunger across the world. Why we more often than not get paid less than men for the same (yes, the very same) work. Why the United Nations reports that women worldwide are more at risk of rape and domestic violence than of cancer or car accidents.[1] Why millions of girls across the globe are actively denied an education. Why we as women must do something significant for the gender to which we belong.

It was a regular day at the office except that International Women's Day[2] was almost upon us. I scrolled through lots of teaser tweets about special events which were planned to mark the day in the United Kingdom and discovered that there was a national call to highlight the impact that women have in the workplace. This was by making our absence felt through a mini strike at lunchtime. The idea was not to disrupt or to cause workplace chaos, but to say, "Hey, without us these jobs wouldn't get done. We're capable and we want fair recognition for that."

Marking the global day of action with more than a pink frosted cake or high fives with my colleagues was very compelling so I set about talking to my female co-workers about how we might do this within our organisation. It was important to me that my colleagues were fully engaged in any activity we decided to do. I talked to lots of women, some on a one to basis and some in small groups. We happily chatted about the growing momentum for International Women's Day and our delight at how many women were joining in with the #westrike event[3] to make a stand across the United Kingdom for each other. I then asked for ideas on what we would like to do to mark the day in the office and show solidarity with each other.

The moment I asked the question was like an ideas high five that isn't returned. There was the glorious tension as my open palm for ideas hung in the air, waiting for a reciprocal high five, and then the awkward lowering of my hand when I realised there would be no high fives, or ideas, for International Women's Day solidarity. Not on that day, anyway.

My females colleagues were happy to chat about gender equality and the need for our empowerment. When it came to taking personal action, to standing up and saying, "I will do this for myself and we will do this for each other," only two women out of a group of about sixty stepped up. When it came to instigating real change I was faced with the passive conviction of women bystanders.

Women who said:

"I believe in your right to do something but it's not for me"

"I'm not a feminist so I'd rather not"

"But women are equal now"

"I believe in women's rights but I'm not in to politics"

"What if we get in trouble? I'm not sure it's worth it"

"It won't achieve anything"

"If you set something up I'll join you but I haven't got time to plan"

"Do you want me to strike so that you can sack me?"

"We could just do a team tweet couldn't we. Do we need to do any more?"

This was the moment I realised why. Taking an active part in the thought leadership of empowerment was not something which most of the women I spoke to that day wanted to do. In fact many were strongly against it stating that feminism was not something they were interested in. The realisation saddened me, but it also showed me how much potential there is for positive change.

And so, I would like to make a bold assertion. That a future of global gender equality, where women are fully equal with men in every single country in the world, depends very much on how women actively stand with each other, fight for each other, encourage each other and empower each other.

It is true that we undoubtedly also need men to consistently be part of the empowerment story and there are many men who have been, and continue to be, catalysts for feminism. Men though, have occupied gender power and not parity for centuries.

Male feminism has not been enough to enable true gender equality within any country across the globe. Men are undoubtedly part of the solution, but throughout history they have also been a very big part of the problem.

I am not asserting that the reason the world is so gender unequal is because of women. Absolutely not. But I am asserting that there is so much more that women can do to further the cause of equality. It is not because of women that so few are on the boards of FTSE 100 (Financial Times Stock Exchange) companies in the UK. It is not because of women that in Russia it is illegal for females to get a job steering a ship. Or that in Madagascar women are banned from working at night, and in Niger that married women can't open a bank account without the permission of their husband.[4]

It is because since the beginning of time, with relatively few social and political exceptions, men have secured and then maintained power for the privilege of their own gender. It is now time for us as women to highlight that privilege, at all levels, and in all societies, in order to actively orbit to a gender equal world. Women empowering women is the change we need to achieve global gender equality.

The world needs concerted change on so many levels to achieve this. Sustainable and significant impact has to begin with the dis-empowered taking back power. After all, power by its very nature is not something which can be given but which must be taken to fully appreciate its significance. Therefore, this book explores how women can empower each other as a catalyst for female and male equality.

Narrating Empowerment

Part 2

Equal and Different

Challenging accepted male norms is an important part of gaining equality. As female beings, we need to empower ourselves to create our own way, rather than adopting the established masculine social, political, economic, and historical norms. Female power does not necessarily have to mimic the established status quo of male power.

Ponder these questions:

- *Can it be possible for someone to lead "like a woman" and yet have the same opportunities as men?*

- *Can a woman "live like a man" if she so chooses without feeling that she has betrayed her sex or her gender?*

- *Is it possible for women and men to be simultaneously equal and different?*

- *Does "difference," either through our sex or our gender, mean that equality cannot be defined or achieved at all?*

Gender equality is about men and women having fair access to opportunities, resources, rights, status and protection. The concept of equal and different is demonstrated well, albeit in different ways, in the starkly contrasting countries of Iceland and Kuwait. Both countries are hugely different; yet each has huge amounts to teach us about equality.

Iceland is a country famed for its stars, its glaciers, its volcanoes and its seasonal patterns of light and darkness as well as its cold weather and its glowing record on gender equality. Kuwait is a country famed for its desert sands, its retail playground, its oil wealth, its Islamic heritage, its extreme heat and its female oppression. To research the content for this book, I travelled from the freezing temperature of Reykjavik to the baking temperature of Kuwait City to find out what the two places have to offer regarding the best practice of women empowering women.

For many years, from the perspective of many lenses, numerous reports and a significant amount of research, Iceland has been esteemed as a leading country in terms of gender equality. It is by far proclaimed the best country in the world for women's safety, women's opportunities, women's pay, and women's rights overall. In contrast, Kuwait is often described as significantly less progressive when it comes to women's rights and yet, despite this, there are some Kuwaiti women who are smashing through the inequality barriers to be the agents of change both for themselves and for other women.[5] It is for these reasons that my travels for this book have taken me to Reykjavik and Kuwait City in particular. It made sense to talk to females who have the support of their legal system and their communities in Iceland, and also to those who have made notable breakthroughs on the gender agenda in Kuwait through more informal means.

I knew that there would be value to be discovered in both countries. The struggle for women's equality is still very much ongoing in both Iceland and Kuwait.

The former may well have an immensely strong track record in equality, but despite this, it still cannot claim gender parity.

Let that sink in. The title of the first country to achieve equality between the genders is sadly still waiting to be claimed.

I wanted to get answers on the way forward to a brighter and equal future, and I was not left disappointed.

To ensure a thorough process for this book I interviewed women across the social, political, geographical, familial and employment spectrums. I had the opportunity to meet with women working in British Embassies outside of the United Kingdom, with politicians, with home makers and with Chief Executives. I was helped by professors, doctors, authors, journalists, mothers, wives, daughters, cleaners, cabin crew, librarians, engineers, architects, home owners, fashion designers and drivers. The majority of my interviews were conducted face to face, but where this wasn't possible then interviews using digital channels took place. Each of the women I had the privilege of speaking to has been formative in the insights shared in this book. Some are directly quoted, and all of the other women have collectively formed the body of research shared here through the very act of communicating their experiences.

The book will major on the insights I gained from Reykjavik and Kuwait City. It will also include learnings from other places I have visited on my empowerment search, including Saudi Arabia,

Pakistan, Oman, The United Arab Emirates, The United States, Canada, Qatar, Germany, France, Italy, Portugal, Spain, Turkey, Singapore and my home country of the United Kingdom.

My written account is intended to be thorough but by no means an academic tome. In completing this work it was important that I heard and shared what the women I spoke to really think, believe and do; not what they think is expected of them. Therefore, some of the women I interviewed have asked to remain anonymous whilst others have been happy to publicly share their stories. I owe a great debt to all of these women, whether kept anonymous or public, as they have been instrumental in empowering others by sharing their experiences, feelings, thoughts and insights.

When an interviewee has asked to be kept anonymous, I have referred to her by first name only (which is sometimes substituted for her real name to preserve confidentiality), but when I have had permission to reference an interviewee or they have spoken at a public forum on the matter concerned then I have used her full name. When women speak up we all benefit; this book is a testimony to scores of women who have taken personal responsibility for instigating change in gender equality.

Throughout the book you will find empowering narratives from women who are everyday activists for a gender equal world. The narratives are interesting snapshots which have been shared when I asked questions about personal experiences of female empowerment. I, and the women who generously shared them, hope that the narratives are useful, inspiring and powerful.

In creating this narrative I am more certain than ever that concerted change needs to start with women empowering women. We are the gender who get a raw deal and for there to be a gender equilibrium then men must give up their gendered privilege. It has to start with us driving change ourselves first, as men have a vested interest in avoiding the challenge of rebalancing the gender equality gap.

You will find practical actions and evidence for women's empowerment throughout the book. Each Other is designed to be read chronologically so that you can see how the practical toolkit for action has been researched; or you can go straight to the complete collection of empowerment actions which have been included as a standalone section at the end. This toolkit section is intended to be referred to and used on a long term basis and I encourage you to contact me to add new actions to the collection over time so that we can tackle the gender equality gap together. Our world continues to change and we must work together to change with it for the betterment of equality for our gender. For those readers who love perusing facts and figures for themselves, I have also included a number of charts and supporting evidence in the appendices which you will find useful.

Now is the time for the gender agenda.

For Each Other: Toolkit Action 1

Take part in collective action ... with heart

Collective female action is crucial for lasting change, be this formally or informally.

The potential for collective activism, and the ensuing results, are well worth investing in both socially and politically. It was the lack of gumption for collective action on International Women's Day, in my own city of Birmingham, that lead me to realise why women are treated unequally.

Together we need to make a stand for equality.

Leaving the hard work to a few individuals will not reap the results which the world needs. Please remember that just turning up because it's the right thing to do is not enough; you need to take part with your whole heart.

For Each Other: Toolkit Action 2

Get social

To pave the way for the next generation of leaders we need to show them that inclusion comes from the top. As leaders, we have a key role in helping females to break out and get to the next level. We need to stand up for women and provide them with new opportunities. In a world filled at the top with men it's important that we don't fall in to the merit trap as this is where bias finds its way in to the selection process. It's important that we have a clear and strong voice when it comes to gender equality.

Advocating for equality means being heard. Use your Twitter feed and Facebook posts to get active in the community and be a strong role model. It's also very useful to girls and women when you are able to be a guest speaker in the classroom, at conferences and at social gatherings. Choose the channels which work best for your story and then get communicating.

For example, my sister is a Doctor and recently ran a session with sixty schoolchildren (boys and girls) on what it is like to be in the medical profession. She also took along a Nurse and a Practice Manager (both female). After the session, the teacher said that the children were buzzing like they had never done before. Not only were they intrigued to find out the gory and gruesome details involved in being a doctor:

- " *Have you ever chopped off the wrong leg (referring to amputations)?*"

- *" What's the grossest thing you've ever done?"*
- *" Is my granny in 'eaven?"*

But it was also good for them to see and hear from women talking about the roles which they do and why they chose them.   One particularly inquisitive child asked, "Why do you each do what you do?"

You could get social by chatting with people face to face or do it on social media.   Twitter is great for sharing news and short, sharp bursts of wisdom. Facebook is great for longer posts and Instagram for images.

If you're doing something feminist that will inspire others to take action, please post it on at least one social network to extend the reach of your message.

How Far We Must Go

Part 3

More Equal is not Enough

We must be clear that being "more equal" in comparison to decades past is not the result which our activism should be moving towards. It is commonplace for people to state that things are okay because they are better than they were. The goal in mind must be "equal" and then the challenge will be to maintain the new equal social balance.

I suspect that the complacent attitude to accepting "more equal" is why women have only recently been granted the legal right to drive in Saudi Arabia; why marital rape was only deemed illegal in the UK in 1992 and why in Malta if a man kidnaps a woman and then forcibly marries her then he becomes exempt from prosecution (albeit this law is now, at last, in the process of being repealed).

Growing up in 1980s Britain was a challenging experience for me, both because of my gender and my race. My active approach to intersectional feminism stems from my early years of fighting for a more equal world. In many ways I cannot deny that my world has become more equal, but it is not completely equal even now.

In school it was always girls and women who were the ones who held me back. I have memories of female classmates in junior school who pushed me in to auditioning for male roles in the annual play because they said I was "long and lanky". Memories of the female English Literature teacher whose classes I adored, who seriously advised me to "become a legal secretary" even though I scored consistent A grades throughout my school years. Memories of the five girls who grabbed my ponytail and pushed my head in to the playground hut toilet so that I lost my brand new hairband in the bowl and then got taunted for being a "toilet head" all afternoon. Where were the boys when the girls were holding each other back (or holding another girl's head in the toilet)? They were passive spectators. They did not empower me but they did not disempower me either like the girls did.

For many reasons, both personal and observed, I feel confident in asserting that we as women need to do more to actively support each other. That we need to stop holding each other back. Passive just doesn't cut it either.

Careless examples of gender equality from adult role models in my youth have long stuck in my mind:

"Margaret Thatcher has shown that women are no longer held back."

"Benazir Bhutto is a symbol of women's empowerment."

Both Thatcher and Benazir normalised the notion of female success to some extent by achieving positions of power which were hard fought for within patriarchal systems. However, neither of the female Prime Ministers showed a dedication to social equality or meaningful female solidarity. It is not enough just to achieve a position of power. That authority must be put to active and responsible use. Symbols of female power are important in normalising and inspiring but being a symbol alone will keep society in a place of "more equal" and not completely equal.

Women have been fighting for their rights for generations, for the right to vote, the right to control our bodies and the right to equality in the workplace. Yet we still have a long way to go, and our victories are under threat. Somehow we seem to have taken on more work by being both home makers and job holders, rather than taking on a fair share of work alongside our male peers. "Having it all," should not mean that we end up doing it all.

Women in a range of fields from domestic work to the entertainment industry, to local and global business, will affirm that equality is still a faraway dream. Being thankful for a "more equal" world will instil a social complacency which could slide us back down the equality scale in time. How far have women really come?

To illustrate the inequality point here are some examples from the United Kingdom since 1918, the year when some, but not all, women were first granted the right to vote.

1919 The Sex Discrimination (Removal) Act
This was the first piece of equal opportunities legislation to officially enter the statute book. For the first time, women could become lawyers, doctors and bank managers. They could also sit on a jury or become a magistrate.

1922 The Law of Property Act
This piece of legislation meant that husbands and wives had equal rights to inherit property from each other. Before this, women were forced to give up all rights to their property when they got married. Prior to this their legal status was on equal ranking to criminals. Then in 1926, new legislation finally gave women the same rights as men to own and dispose of property.

1923 The Matrimonial Causes Act
This act allowed women to petition for divorce if their husband had been unfaithful. Before the act was passed, only men were allowed to divorce their wife due to adultery.

1967 The NHS (Family Planning) Act
This act was important for a number of reasons. Firstly, it made contraception available to all women; previously the service had only been granted to those whose health would be endangered by pregnancy. Secondly, it made it legal for local health authorities to give family planning advice to unmarried women.

1970 Equal Pay Act
This act made it illegal to pay women less than men for the same amount of work. It also made it illegal to give women less favourable conditions of employment than men. I was very surprised when I learned of this legislation given the current gender pay gap in the UK.

1975 The Employment Protection Act
This made it illegal to fire women for being pregnant. The legislation also established that women were

entitled to take maternity leave, and that they had the right to return to their position.

1990 Independent taxation introduced
Women were not taxed independently from their husbands until 1990. At the time of writing this book, that is just twenty eight years ago. This law finally marked their income as their own, rather than as an addition to their husband's earnings.

1991 Rape within marriage became a crime
Before this date it was legal for a man to rape his wife. It took another ten years after this ruling for the word "consent" to finally be given a legal definition, under the 2003 Sexual Offences Act. Anyone who thinks that the UK is a progressive country for women needs to be reminded that this was less than thirty years ago.

2018 Gender pay gap widely highlighted
All companies employing more than 250 staff were called upon to declare the gender pay gaps between men and women in an effort to expose pay inequalities.

Each year women have driven social, political and economic change to become more equal. But that just isn't enough anymore. Many women are done with hoping for things to change, asking for things to change and campaigning for things to change. We now need to achieve the plot twist we deserve for ourselves and with each other. It is time to hold ourselves to account.

For Each Other: Toolkit Action 3

Encouraging women to infantilise men has got to stop

In order to help ourselves as well as each other we must stop infantilising men.

Is there really a good reason why women are trying to do it all and carrying the mental load even when we physically don't need to? Saying, "It's just quicker when I do it," or "He doesn't do it quite the way I would" does not cut it. Women have lost all sight of their empowerment perspective when they say it's easier if they do everything themselves. Really? Easier for who exactly? Is there really such a wrong way of loading up the dishwasher or putting away the supermarket shop? And what makes women better at doing the ironing anyway?

Women have to stop treating men like infants and men have to stop pretending that they can't do things and pandering to infantilisation.

I once met a woman who confessed that after she returned to work post maternity leave, she would dash home at lunchtimes when her husband was on baby duty as, "He just can't change the nappy poor thing no matter how hard he tries." Instead of taking a hard earned refreshment break she dashed home in the car to swap a dirty nappy for a clean one to last the afternoon until she got home from work again. Her husband was more than happy to let her do this.

There is an advert on air in the UK this year which shows a male and female married couple and their baby. The mum goes out to work and programs their intelligent home speaker to give her husband timely reminders to help him out with his baby care duties. The speaker reminds the husband that a playdate has been arranged for the afternoon, where various food stuffs are kept and finally, that the husband is "doing a great job" and is loved by his wife. The advert is promoting sales of the speaker and sadly normalises the sphere of the home and bringing up children as that of the mother, with the husband stepping in and "doing a great job" as if it was never his responsibility in the first place. The advert is a disappointment to watch and I am left wondering why and how somebody very senior would have signed off the advert as suitable to air.

For Each Other: Toolkit Action 4

Hold to account

Gender parity needs to be kept firmly on the agenda. We must encourage our own leaders to keep discussing it and measuring it. Proper commitment is needed from Chief Executives and senior leadership teams. At the very least, we should set ourselves and others within our teams the challenge to clearly demonstrate what we have actively done to support women in the workplace. Challenging, recording, monitoring, measuring and communicating will create the initial ripple of actions needed for enticing greater change.

I once suggested in a senior leadership team meeting at a past employer that we needed to actively do more to eradicate the organisation's culture of sexism and racism. Everyone agreed that it needed to be done, "But not now — we just don't have the time," was the general consensus. It would have been easy to stop lobbying for change by telling myself that at least I had tried. But change doesn't happen that way and the right thing to do is to hold to account and engage further. And that's exactly what I did. Getting buy in for issues which many people are complacent about is difficult.

All I know is that the result will be worth it .... in the end.

Hear From Hanifa Shah

Hanifa Shah lives and works in the UK. She is a Professor, a Pro-Vice-Chancellor and the Executive Dean for the Faculty of Computing at Birmingham City University. She has a PhD from the University of Aston in Birmingham, a Masters from Cambridge University and a first class BSc Honours degree in Computing Science from Staffordshire University. Hanifa said:

"My favourite achievement was going to university and getting sponsored by the company Cadbury Schweppes. Certainly no one in my wider family went to University at the time; not even any of the men.

My parents were immigrants who struggled with their life in the UK. My father worked in a factory and my mother had not had any formal education. I grew up in inner city Birmingham in what would now be recognised as extreme poverty. English was not the language spoken in my home so I arrived at my first day in primary school not being able to speak any English words at all. My life overall was impacted by not only the disadvantages of immigration, but also the disadvantages of poverty and being female. In that context, getting to a point where I was able to secure university sponsorship from a company like Cadbury Schweppes via a very competitive process and getting a first class degree in a subject like computing was game changing for me and my family. In my early career there were not many women around to support me as my subject was very male dominated. I'm afraid this has been the case for much of my career.

But there are three groups of women who did actively support me. Many of my primary school teachers were strong independent women so I absorbed some of their strength. I went to an all girls secondary school as a teenager. It was a difficult period in secondary education generally with much of the teaching focussed on bookwork which was sometimes boring and a little suffocating for me. However, being in a school where I was encouraged to excel at sport and being surrounded by girls and mainly female teachers gave me a sense of being able to take part in anything without it being thought of as something only boys did. The other women who empowered me were those who were studying with me when I did computing at university. Despite being in a minority we formed a largely female study group and would allocate each other topics to understand in more detail in order to coach one another. This created a really safe, supportive environment in which we could feel comfortable admitting we didn't know things but were prepared to learn from each other.

I've always shared my knowledge. I have provided advice to others in my community and many of these were young girls from similar backgrounds to my own. It was important to me to help them realise that having an education is important for themselves and their families. Providing practical help with understanding their schoolwork and preparing them for their exams was very useful for them. This was well back before the internet existed. There would be no one they could turn to in their families or at school. Some of the young women that I helped went on to become human rights lawyers, doctors, teachers and social activists. They have also empowered me as they *have been generous in acknowledging my help and support. Giving people your time when you don't have to is a really important thing to do.*

Women often lack resources, especially when combined with other circumstances. The most significant disabler for me wasn't that I was a woman, but that I was growing up in poverty and for much of my early life I didn't have access to financial resources to help me to develop my career.

In order to be successful I urge all women to be prepared to form new networks and collaborative opportunities, but also to take part in existing support groups. As long as we don't become complacent about the women's movement it will continue to show strength and promise. Confident, empowered women will make the world a stronger place."

Men are doing well; imagine how much better our planet could be if women were enabled to do just as well.

Hear from Dunya

Dunya is a television producer at one of Kuwait's major news shows. She is responsible for the content of the show by sourcing people to interview who can provide specialist views on the big stories of the day. Her selection of interviewees is critical in the views and perspectives that are put across for the Kuwaiti audiences watching the show at home. Working on a news programme is always fast paced and extremely highly pressured, and as a result it is quite common for producers to use the comfort of their little trusted book of contacts when enlisting the help of experts to be interviewed.

This approach has caused a number of gender equality issues for Dunya. She could make life easy for herself and take some of the pressure off her workload by going to the old favourites for TV interviews. Whenever she looked for new experts, like someone to talk about the emerging trends in robotics, the interviewees available were nearly always male. The challenges she faced were two fold. Firstly, the expert had to be a genuine specialist and in Kuwait there was still a lot of work to be done to improve gender representation across the labour spectrum. Secondly, the time pressure of finding someone to comment, sometimes with only a few hours notice meant that it was almost impossible to source female representation.

When it came to experts on television women were still being hidden away. This was particularly so when it came to political or economic stories. Other producers were happy enough if there was a woman featured every now and again to show that women were at least now being represented as more equal. But for Dunya that wasn't enough.

"I was getting fed up of arranging for the same men to be interviewed as experts for TV year in, year out. There's one economic expert who has been appearing on our show for over six years. Surely we could have found even one woman to interview in all that time!"

So she decided to take action and compile her own lists of female experts, in an attempt to counter the argument that female voices are just not out there. She used Instagram and Snapchat as a route to finding them — these are channels where women in Kuwait are already sharing their opinions and having live debates about the big topics of the day.

Dunya's TV programme now has a big trusted book of women experts to rely on. It's not always easy to get people who haven't self selected to come on TV to take a seat on the newsroom sofa, but at least now there's the daily opportunity to increase female representation.

In Arabic, "Dunya" means "world". Slowly but surely, the Kuwaiti view on female empowerment is changing for the betterment of our world.

Hear from Madison

Madison is a successful business woman working for one of Canada's highest turnover retail companies. She has always been a high performer at work and has been headhunted on three separate occasions for career promotions in rival companies.

Well known in the retail industry, she believes that it is her duty to speak out for other women and make it known that she is an active female cheerleader, *"But not the pom pom kind of cheerleader,"* she asserts.

She received a call one day from a female headhunter who told Madison that given her experience and strong reputation, a competing retailer would be delighted if Madison applied to join their Board as Operations Director. The company concerned was on the lookout for someone who was not only a strong business performer, but also someone who was confident in getting gender on the retailer's agenda. The headhunter pitched the company as highly progressive and evidenced this by their recently made commitment, "To ensure that twenty per cent of the Board is female within three years".

Madison was dumbstruck.

She thinks she may have even internally chortled at this audaciously unambitious target. It was hard for her to decide what had infuriated her most. Whether it was the fact that a female headhunter had thought that such an insignificant target would appeal to her, or that a company who professed they were progressive actually thought that twenty per cent female representation on a Board was enough.

To make matters worse, when Madison declined to apply for the role, the headhunter asked her if she could recommend anyone else who would be suitable. *"I don't know any women who would settle for that ethos,"* she said.

Sadly, the headhunter still didn't understand the implications of Madison's message and asked, "It doesn't have to be a woman although a woman would be ideal. Perhaps you could recommend a man you know who would be good for the job?"

Madison knew that more equal was not enough. Her headhunter and the company she was recruiting for, however, still had this to learn in order not to actively disempower other women.

Exploring Feminism

Part 4

Global Female Leaders

Berlin. A city that has in centuries past been a leader in human disempowerment is now ardently working towards being at the forefront of human empowerment. The Brandenburg Gate is a monument which has come to symbolise peace and unity for Germany. A symbol which not only reminds us of the East and West divide, but then also it's glorious reunification in 1990.

It was here that I had arranged to meet a number of global female leaders who, like me, were heading to Berlin to connect with each other and find practical ways to end the gender equality gap. Women leaders were heading to the Brandenburg Gate on a mission to both empower others and be empowered themselves.

When I arrived at Berlin airport, I was happy to discover that my pre-booked taxi driver was a woman. Bernadette found my delight at her arrival rather amusing and so we chatted about gender bias within the transport industry. She explained that being assigned the pick up from the airport that day was a rarity and that preference was normally given to her male colleagues. She was the only female driver in her taxi firm in the city and so it was hard to prove that she was held back from the most profitable airport run jobs because of her gender, but most of her colleagues got at least one airport run a day whilst she got on average just one a month. My journey with Bernadette suited me so much more than journeys with male drivers I have taken in the past. It was just a taxi ride, but she totally understood what I needed to be comfortable and that got my trip off to a brilliant start.

The conversation I had with Bernadette also got me thinking about the taxi rides I have taken in other countries and how basic transportation can do so much to empower or disempower women. In Dubai, there is a road transport initiative which allows women passengers to be driven by a female if they so choose. The taxis are identified by a pink roof to make them easier to spot. I was very excited when I first discovered this but then, after chatting with a number of pink taxi drivers, I found that they were hugely disempowered compared to their male peers.

In the main, pink taxis can only be booked in advance or taken from the pink taxi rank at the airport. Whenever I arrive at Dubai airport I am adamant that I want a taxi with a female driver but it's not always that easy to achieve even though there are normally at least fifty pink taxis waiting for passengers. The pink rank is the last in the suite of taxi ranks, lined up after the "standard" taxis which are all driven by males and after the luxury limousine taxis, again all driven by males.

I have always had to tussle with the concierge to make my way to the pink rank. They have always tried to usher me to a luxury taxi first, then a standard one, and it's only if I tackle them head on and ask them to let me pass to the pink rank that I make it through. For the female taxi drivers themselves there's also then another challenge; the size of their market is so much smaller than their male colleagues. Whilst males can drive men, women and families, female drivers can only drive women and families. If you are a woman travelling in Dubai I beseech you to make every effort to take a pink taxi. It may well be the only ride that driver gets on the day. I can imagine that you might well be thinking that the male taxi drivers aren't well off either; that they're also working hard to earn a living and that many of them will be supporting their children (some who will be girls) to go to school, buy them clothes and provide safe accommodation. This is true, most of the taxi drivers, whether male or female in Dubai, have emigrated to earn the little money which they couldn't have ever dreamed of earning in their homelands. The fact remains though that the male taxi drivers have more opportunity to earn on a daily basis.

But now, back to Berlin.[6] I was on my way to soak up a serious dose of empowerment in one of the world's greatest cities. I felt somehow that when I got to the Gate, I would be on the precipice of being transformed.

When I arrived I was not disappointed. The meeting was packed with over two hundred female leaders, the majority of whom had hard won the titles of CEO, Chair, President, Vice President, Director or quite simply, Entrepreneur.

The concept of leadership was front of mind for all of us, and intertwined with this we could not ignore how digitalisation and technological developments, along with a changing political and demographic landscape, had catapulted the world in to a new age of disruption.

One of the first women I met on the day was Susan from State Street Global Advisers in the USA. Susan was very clear that despite the evidence linking gender diversity to long term value, women are still under represented in corporate leadership. She backed up her assertion with a report published by her organisation which found that companies with stronger female leadership perform better and experience less fraud, bribery and shareholder conflict.[7] This outperformance is largely attributed to the independent perspectives women bring to the boardroom. State Street Global Advisers is in the business of money, and the gender equality conundrum is a financial issue which they take very seriously. Without a doubt, gender diversity in corporate leadership will yield better financial performance.

The conversation led me to think hard about how and why I invest. When I invest in stocks and shares I think about the potential financial returns I could make and base decisions on the likelihood of positive financial outcomes. I mitigate my risk and ensure that I have a diversified investment portfolio. So why then, does society not take the same approach when investing in people? Why are companies so male heavy? And in Europe why are companies so focussed on white males in particular? If for no other reason than a positive return, diversifying our people investment portfolio has to be a good thing.

One of the most highly achieved and resoundingly inspiring women I met during the trip was Roya Mahboob. It would seem unlikely to many people that a quiet and self-confessed shy woman from

Afghanistan would be a keynote speaker at events across the globe. In 2013, she was named one of TIME magazine's "100 Most Influential People"[8] for her work in building digitised classrooms for girls in Afghanistan. In a country where it is a rarity for women to work outside of the home, Roya established herself as a strong businesswoman, CEO and global female mentor. Despite facing a number of death threats for her work, in 2010 she set up the Afghan Citadel Software Company to create jobs for female university graduates in her country. She was a woman who had empowered herself, and she felt it her duty and her calling to go on and empower other women to live happy and fulfilled lives.

Roya's accomplishments are many, but for me her magnetism comes from a genuine desire to provide women with practical solutions through which they can apply themselves and grow. She now runs her own company called the Digital Citizen Fund[9] which is teaching girls about bit coin and block chain technology. Through empowering women with practical support she has also enabled a number of them to help their entire families, including overcoming the pushback and sexism they have faced from men, many of whom have been close family members. One girl in Roya's programme overcame the impact of the harsh criticisms of her father and went on to set up her own Afghan based business. The business has been so successful that it now employs all of her family members, including her ex-problematic father who is now a full on advocate and productive colleague on the payroll.

As I listened, I realised that Roya's journey was full of challenges which I myself had never had to confront. Yet she had faced the challenges, conquered them, and empowered not only herself but others too. Imagine running a company where most of your staff don't even have a bank account; how could they get paid in a safe and secure way? Roya was a joy to listen to. She said, "In any society women are not yet equal. Technology can change this. It changed my world."

Digital change can certainly be enabling, but it did lead me to wonder whether technology in male hands can beget fair rewards for women? Can it be true that technology may well be unequally gendered? Perhaps even subliminally gendered so that the results are even more dangerous to equality than anyone could have imagined? To explore this theme further I spoke to Stacia from the German digital platform called Zalando.[10] It was enlightening to hear from Stacia as she has been close to the development of Artificial Intelligence and its impact on gender. She asserted that AI is an enabler for humans and not a replacement. "We think that machines are not biased," she said, "but that in itself is biased." I learned that algorithmic bias is pervasive. It is everywhere and affects pretty much everything. There are many examples of poor product design caused by product test bias.

Artificial intelligence and design bias is problematic when it comes to gender, race, ethnicity, socioeconomic class, sexual orientation and more. For example, Google's computer vision system shockingly labelled African-Americans as gorillas, while Microsoft's vision system was reported to fail to recognise darker-skinned people. Unfortunately, when a single homogeneous group is designing and engineering the vast majority of technology, they will consciously and unconsciously pass on their own biases. Imagine the implications for self driving cars. Will gender or race affect life or death decisions made by machines which are programmed by humans transferring their bias?

Using flawed data sets or biased data sets for product development, and particularly for AI, poses a risk to feminism. It could actually mean that in some areas women's opportunities go backwards. The concept of female servitude is also rising through technology such as through the female voices and female names of technological personal assistants like Amazon's Alexa. These digital assistants are embodying gender stereotypes as the robots have female voices by default and are designed to carry out mainly assistance and subservience roles. Yes, it is true that the voices can be changed to male ones, but how often have you come across someone who has changed the voice on their digital assistant to sound male? I can't think of even one example from within my own network.

When chat bots and voice assistants are programmed by male coders then it should come as no surprise that machines can perpetuate inequalities found in the real world. This can have unintended consequences, and perhaps even worse consequences than inequalities which are directly delivered from humans. This is because we often hold the false belief that machines have no bias. The solution, perhaps, is to provide a gendered development of this space which is transparent, since transparency will help overcome bias, and provide a purposefully diverse community which includes gender and the full spectrum of multicultural perspectives.

However, there is also another view. Ersilia from the European Space Agency believes that gendering in robots is unnecessary.[11] She asserts that empathy and listening will become even more important in the future because of how language carries implicit information such as feelings, environmental context and social subtexts. All of these elements are implicit in language and therefore language is so much more than the construction of words and grammar alone. Awareness of societal bias is important. Is there really a need to create the bias in robots she asks?

The two differing points of view on the gendering of robots and artificial intelligence are united in their view of risks for gender inequality and the potential for equality. Either way, we do not have parity now and so we must make sure that we work towards achieving clear parity in the future. Transparency of opinion, transparency of leadership and transparency of implementation will be enablers in a gender equal future.

For Each Other: Toolkit Action 5

Provide platforms where women can learn

Women who are breaking through social, political and economic barriers can support others by creating workgroups, coaching new leaders and providing safe platforms where they can learn from their mistakes and those of others. Paving a path to leadership by those already in senior positions is key to encouraging a new and diverse generation of employees.

There are lots of formal and informal ways in which you can do this. Such as:

- Mentoring or sponsoring someone.

- Arranging a networking group where women can meet on a regular basis.

- Matchmaking for leadership (not for love)! If you know a woman who would benefit from getting to know a friend or colleague of yours then introduce them.

- Be a cheerleader for fellow females when they do something well.

- Point out mistakes in private so that people can learn. It's hard to give not-so-positive feedback but when you really care about someone it's important. Keep in mind that some situations may require public feedback (handled sensitively of course) so that others can learn too.

- Set up an event where the women at work can get together and talk about issues. I currently work at a co-operative which did this. The President and our only female C-suite executive spoke about their personal and career journeys which had a profound effect on so many women who attended. The event caused some tension with the men as it was a women only event so it's essential to make sure that you head this off and explain why this is necessary.

- Set up a Facebook group or a Whatsapp group for women across various leadership levels to stay in touch.

- Write a blog about your feminist learning experiences — you can always use a pseudonym if you wish.

- Pass on books you've read to other women so that they can learn from them too.

Providing platforms for others to learn is easy. We can all change the world in our own way.

Hear from Aldijana Sisic

The Tower of London is a castle steeped in history located on the north bank of the River Thames in the United Kingdom's capital city. It was here that a Gala Dinner was hosted by the United Nations Trust Fund to End Violence Against Women [12]. It was an evening to raise funds for the cause, raise further awareness of the issues, network amongst like minded people, and above all to *"friend raise"*.

Aldijana Sisic, the Chief of the United Nations Trust Fund to End Violence Against Women, gave a rousing speech, acknowledging that the evening was not just about raising funds, but also about making new friends ("friend raising"), working together with existing friends, and being active friends to women and girls around the world who are in need of our help. She was also adamant that the reduction of violence against women was just not enough. It would never be okay to say that three per cent, two per cent or even one per cent of women were at the receiving end of violence. It would only be okay to say zero per cent; when every woman and every girl could confidently live a life of safety.

It was revealed on the night that almost thirty five per cent of women worldwide have experienced either physical or sexual intimate partner violence or sexual violence by a non-partner at some point in their lives. However, some national studies show that up to seventy per cent of women have experienced physical or sexual violence from an intimate partner in their lifetime.[12]

Aldijana's call is for female equality through female solidarity.

Who can you friend raise with?

Hear from Valerie Dwyer

Valerie is an Entrepreneur, a Coach and Author of the book, "Woman Power: Strategies for Female Leaders". An active champion for women's enterprise all of her career, the UK Government appointed her to the Women's Enterprise Taskforce to create an environment for more women to start and grow businesses.

She said, *"Issues that we often do not think about in relation to women's empowerment are within women themselves. Issues of mindset, of belief, courage and confidence. I have experienced first-hand, many times, how by contributing to building these qualities we empower others. Women's empowerment means ensuring access to the right education, information, knowledge and resources to understand the world and our place within it. To make informed choices and know that we ourselves have the power to create exactly the life we want."*

"Whenever you step up in life" Valerie says, *"leave the ladder down and help other women up with you."* [13]

We're In It Together

Part 5

The Problem with Privilege

So far, my research on women's empowerment was going well in Berlin. I'd heard many new views which I had not considered before. One morning, the opportunity arose to have breakfast with a few women leaders who wanted to discuss the concept of gender and empowerment with a focus on practical steps we could take to help each other.

Ten of us met in a beautiful orangery in the Hotel Adlon Kempinski which is within touching distance of the Brandenburg Gate. On arrival, a few of my new acquaintances were reminiscing about The Ritz where they met for a chat last year. One of the ladies pulled me straight in to the conversation and said, "The Adlon is adequate, and it may well be the place where Obama stays when he's in Berlin, but The Ritz is so much better. It's much nicer to chat in comfortable surroundings, don't you think?" I wasn't able to comment as I hadn't been to The Ritz in Berlin, neither had I stayed at The Adlon overnight. I had checked myself in to a local hotel which was a fifth of the price of the one I was sitting in now. In fact, truth be told I had found the Adlon so jaw droppingly luxurious that I had to work really hard to keep my poise and not take any selfies in the golden gilded lounge the day before, where a cup of tea was the price of a bottle of high end eau de parfum. I had wanted to whoop with delight at the gaudy beauty of the place (and I would have done had I been alone).

When I shared that I had stayed at a standard business hotel the night before there were many looks of confusion around the breakfast table. "Never mind honey," said one of the women, "like I said it's not as good as The Ritz anyway. You must check that out next time you're in Berlin." Nobody seemed to understand that the hotel which the conference was in could be seen as an unnecessary expense for many people.

We soon began our empowerment exchange in earnest. Anna, an investment banker, had worked in China for five years before returning to her native home in Switzerland. Her perception was that in China there are more female leaders than other parts of the world because home help was still readily accessible and exceptionally cheap. "In China," Anna said, "women can focus on their careers as housework is easily taken care of. I had a live-in nanny to look after my daughter as well as a cleaner who did a daily shift and she even prepared the ingredients for my family meals."

The domestic help removed a lot of the burdens associated with daily life for Anna without the need to engage her husband in taking a fair share of the housework and child care responsibilities. It meant that she was able to thrive at work and gained two promotions in five years. Two other women in the room had also lived in China and had the privilege of hiring help, more often than not the home help candidates were women, and more often than not these women lived in their employer's home.

The impact on a woman's career who has such a stable source of support at home is undoubtedly a great help in securing her own career advantage. I couldn't help but wonder though, how this was perhaps about women with racial and financial privilege taking the opportunity to empower themselves through working around gender inequality. Sure enough, Anna had empowered other women by giving them employment as live-in home help. But did this really help less financially privileged women in the long run? Did it even help her own personal case for gender equality with her husband? Was she inadvertently perpetuating gender and racial inequalities further?

Wouldn't it be more empowering for our daughters, our sisters, our female friends and our female colleagues if we all took a stand and worked harder at holding men to account for their responsibility in the domestic sphere? Could buying in home help, which is generally female home help, be perpetuating the problem of gender inequality in countries like China? It seemed to me that not only could it increase the gender equality gap, but also the wealth gap across societal classes.

To empower each other surely we need to stand side by side rather than on the shoulders of other women to advance our own careers? The fact that female "home help is cheap" in China and other countries in itself is a problem, highlighting the hostage wages that many women are forced to work for at the expense of their own personal families and life balance.[14] The problem with privilege, particularly financial privilege, is that it can make us lazier in thinking about sustainable and equitable solutions to the gender equality conundrum. Sometimes we might even use it to hold other women back without even realising what we have done. I love a good hotel as much as anyone I breakfasted with that day, but I was also keenly aware that it was the quality of the conversation that would count and that this could be as productive as we chose it to be, whether it was at The Ritz, The Adlon, or a business hotel.

There was also a big and uncomfortable element of exclusion in our conversation. The delegates had all made the decision to conference together in Berlin and flown in from various countries to meet in one of the grandest hotels in the city where the fee to get in to the conference was several thousand euros. Everyone in attendance was wealthy enough, accomplished enough or lucky enough to have gained funding, but in doing so, we were excluding female voices who did not have the same financial accessibility.

I was in Berlin to learn from leading female business women about how we could empower each other. That day, I had uncomfortably heard how I could empower myself through low paid home staff if I so wished. One of my acquaintances was also restlessly wriggling on her seat whilst she listened. Her name was Elena and she was due to retire in six months time. She had spent her entire career in Germany working in finance and was a keen women's advocate.

Elena explained that in her company she had worked for over a decade to gain engagement from the Board to implement what she described as a "comply or explain" culture. She said that in Germany there were quotas in place for the number of women expected to be placed in senior positions and that this was making a significant difference. However, as the progress being seen was due to a very recent change in company rules there was a severe lack of women in the succession pipeline across all levels. This made it easier for senior male colleagues to say, "We've looked to make female appointments but there just aren't any out there who want the jobs that we have."

The comply or explain culture was a way of finding out what the declared reasons were when women weren't present at the board table which then allowed directors to get involved and provide support to senior managers on how to overcome the issues that were being faced.

One of the directors at Elena's company had hired a coach to independently explore the biases of male interviewers in the organisation and what they expected as good interview answers. The coach found that women were being screened out of the process, not because they weren't up to the job, but because they didn't answer the interview questions in the way that male candidates did which was the unconscious preference (and even more sadly sometimes conscious preference) for the male interviewers.

Elena's wit was awe inspiringly sharp and her observations of corporate life had led her to the very clear conclusion that as women we are holding ourselves back because we invest much more in human capital (that is, learning about others) than social capital (that is, the sponsoring of others). We were told that women are more likely to listen, watch and learn whereas men actively develop their networks for their own benefit and that of more junior male members of their teams.

The problem with privilege, whether it's financial privilege, gendered privilege, racial privilege or any other kind of privilege, is that it can (if we don't try hard enough at least) stop us from seeing what is right there in front of us. A woman could be waving her arms in front of a male interviewer in some cases and oftentimes he would be able to say that he honestly did not see her.

Privilege can block our view without us even knowing it. I can make this assertion with confidence based on my own personal experience of discussing recruitment with a number of male recruiters. One such male leader is a senior manager in a large retail company I once worked at. I have a huge amount of respect for him as he has a brain bigger than any I've come across before.

We had a debate over lunch one day on the topic of recruitment as we had just been involved in streaming a YouTube video on the subject of gender equality. Benjamin was adamant that quotas, or "positive discrimination" as he called it was not something he thought our organisation should ever entertain.

"People should get the job based on merit, otherwise how will we ever get the best people for the job?" he said. "I just don't believe in positive discrimination."

It was always going to be an awkward debate because I don't believe in the traditional interpretation of "positive discrimination" either. Candidates should only be given a role because they deserve it through the skills and experience they have to offer. But what if their skills and experience are overlooked because they come in different packaging to the one expected? Just like the coach Elena told us about, there are many male interviewers who screen out women without even realising that it is gender which has influenced their decision. Often people talk about unconscious bias as a way of making their discriminations sound palatable. Unconscious discrimination is not okay.

A couple of years ago I had been successful in gaining a newly created senior manager position at my current company. Had I not been successful, I would have faced redundancy, and in this particular instance the other candidate who was through to the final interview stage was a man. I was so happy when I found out I had gained the role as it truly was a dream job for me. Then, the slap came. I felt humiliated a few days later when I heard that two of my peers, also senior managers within the company, believed that I had secured the role as a result of positive racial discrimination. This was not in the slightest bit true but it hurt nonetheless to think that there were people who couldn't see my skills and experience even though I had been vehemently waving my arms and proving I had what it took. The experience made me realise that anyone who secures a role through quotas has an even harder equality gap to overcome than I did.

I put some current newsworthy examples to Benjamin and asked, "You've received positive discrimination all of your life and benefitted from it through faster career progression, better pay, stronger networks and better social opportunities because you are male. Sure, you've worked hard, you're one of the smartest people I know and you're highly skilled, but your male privilege got you to where you are much faster and that's society's way of positively discriminating in favour of men. Is it so wrong to redress the gender balance engineering to offer the same opportunities for females? Is that even positive discrimination or is it purely an act of social equality and balance which men and women have been unable to work out without quotas being in place?"

Benjamin was confused and couldn't understand why I thought he had male privilege. That in itself is why privilege can be such a big problem to overcome. When men understand that these often invisible perks aren't available to everyone, they will see why addressing privilege means recognising that men and women deserve equal access to basic respect for our humanity. The merit trap is dangerous.

But this book is not about how men can empower women but how women can empower each other. To that end I think it important that we don't shy away from structured quotas or support. It's not positive discrimination if it's redressing a social imbalance which has no way of being rectified otherwise. When as women we say we don't believe in quotas for women then all we are doing is holding each other back. When society is a place of equality, and offers full respect for men and women, then gender quotas will be unnecessary. Until then, it's important that we use the social capital that Elena talked about and sponsor each other to take those senior positions even when this is through quotas.   Personally, I like the, "comply or explain" approach.

Elena presented a very compelling argument for progressing women's confidence in what she called "social capital" over "human capital":

"How many times have you been left out of a critical conversation at work because your boss decided he wanted to chat about it on the golf course? For me, it's happened too many times and the men who are out there on the golf course are getting the sponsorship they need from the boss to move up to the next level."

She was right, of course. The male leaders involved won't even have realised the privilege they have granted their junior male colleagues, they will have seen it as a purely social activity with no career equity attached to it.   Yet the real outcomes of the golf course say otherwise.

Male privilege has frustrated me for much of my life. So I asked my acquaintances at the breakfast meeting to share personal examples of their experiences of this so we might discuss how we could tackle the issues to collectively empower each other. The examples came fast. There are far too many to explore here but I will share a few.

Social norms allow men to take up more physical space perpetuating gender inequality.   All of us without exception had been on train journeys where we had sat ourselves down next to a man, and he had continued to be guilty of leaving his body spread across on to a part of the seat next to him; the seat that we had perched ourselves on waiting for him to retract the man spread. None of us had ever asked the men to move across off our seats and instead we had borne the discomfort. We agreed that to empower each other we needed to ensure we were vocal about our own space, for our own sake and the sake of women who would sit in seats next to the same men after us.

Men can buy clothes designed for their gender that have pockets which they can actually use. Clothes meant for women are often focused on being "slimming," so purely decorative pockets or impractical pockets are commonplace. Those of us who are fortunate enough to be in the business of designing fashion have a responsibility to empower our fellow women. As a footwear designer, all of my heels are super comfortable to offer practicality as well as style. I do not believe that women should have to wear heels; but if they choose to, the least I can do is make them the most comfortable heels they will ever wear. It's hard enough making it to the board room so the least I can do is to empower women through super empowered heels.

Men can forgo regular grooming during travel, like growing a "backpacker's beard". Women are judged for not keeping up with their gender's societal expectations, like shaving their legs. Whether you shave your legs on holiday or not, whether you choose to shave them at all at home or when away, we all decided that the really empowered thing to do was not to behave apologetically about it or gingerly hide ourselves away. Everyone in the room was immaculately groomed and we were all staying away from home. But the point wasn't about the presence of leg hair, it was more about embracing our authentic selves and wearing our personal decisions with pride.

Common vocabulary favours the male gender as the default. Consider language like "mankind" and "chairman". The World Cup for football is a brilliant example of male privilege being normalised. It should not be called the "World Cup" when it includes only men as its players; it should be the "Men's World Cup" alongside the "Women's World Cup". As women we can empower each other by drawing attention to these inequalities and then offering linguistic alternatives. A fabulously gutsy acquaintance of mine called Ashleigh Millman recently drew attention to the issue during the World Cup in Russia during 2018. England, much to everyone's surprise, made it to the semi-finals and the mainstream media, including the BBC (which proclaims itself as impartial) glorified the match as, "The first time in 28 years that England have made it to the World Cup semi-finals." Ashleigh was absolutely right when she tweeted, "Boggling discovery: It is not 28 years since England made a World Cup semi final, it's 3. It's just 28 years since men did".[15] The tweet didn't go viral, but then revelations of male privilege rarely do when it comes to social justice or even social media justice.

Perceptions of how much a gender is represented is biased in favour of men. When a group is comprised of seventeen per cent women, men think it's fifty-fifty, and at thirty three per cent, men believe women are the majority. These statistics were shared by Julia, a Human Resources Director from the USA who was keenly aware of male privilege through her corporate role as well as her personal social experiences.

We had established that male privilege was prevalent in our everyday lives and agreed that investing in social capital was certainly a way in which we could support and empower each other. Interactions linked with social capital are marked by reciprocity, trust and co-operation. Active sponsorship of women by women is key in progressing gender equality.

Active leadership at a senior level is the most significant of all to get us started. This is one of the reasons why when I talked about Margaret Thatcher and Benazir Bhutto at the beginning of the book, I referred to them as careless examples of feminism. Had the two female Prime Ministers actively sponsored and supported the empowerment of even a handful of women they could have made a huge impact in closing the gender equality gap. As it was, their appointments as the leading ministers were good as single statements of feminism but not as sustainable examples. In fact, I have yet to hear any woman or girl say that they think of Thatcher or Bhutto as inspiring feminist role models. Both women have been revered for other stances, skills and achievements. Women's empowerment, however, is not one of them.

It was at the end of our breakfast session that the clearest piece of advice was offered and united everybody in knowing smiles. Irene, a Director of Corporate Responsibility said, "If you must have a male partner then choose him very carefully, he will either make your life easier or harder."

Women coming together around shared concerns have been an important impetus behind struggles for gender equality across the globe.   It's time to take coming together more seriously and make it an integrated part of our everyday lives.

For Each Other: Toolkit Action 6

Take a chance

There are many examples of women in senior leadership positions who have been fortunate in that someone has taken a chance on them. Women can often feel that they are not deserving of a role when in fact they are; or they may not be ready for a role but would get there quickly with the right support.

When you spot someone who you believe could make it but isn't quite ready, take a chance on them. Give them the support and mentoring they need to become the next senior female leader in your organisation. The impact will be felt for generations to come as she will undoubtedly do the same for someone else. Waiting for "the right time" has not gotten women anywhere very fast so far, so it's time to take that chance on yourself and on someone else.

I've sometimes appointed people to a job and it sadly hasn't worked out for them (this includes males and females). But there are many other times when it has worked out amazingly well. You won't always get it right, but it's worth the mistakes for the times when you see someone flourish in a role which they wouldn't have achieved if you hadn't taken a chance on them.

For Each Other: Toolkit Action 7

Look, look and look again

Women are less likely to apply for positions than males with the equal amount of knowledge, skills and experience. When shortlisting for interviews and there are no female candidates (in my experience within senior leadership in retail there often aren't) then it's important to consider whether the roles are being advertised in the right spaces, whether active approaches can be made to females with the required credentials, or even whether they have been screened out through gender bias. Some organisations are starting to use CV screening where the names are not made visible to employers to address gender bias (although that's not the only gender signal).

To ensure that women are being given a fair chance, if the shortlist isn't balanced then look, look and look again.

Hear from Roxanna

Roxanna is in the privileged position of owning a portfolio of apartments in Iceland which she lets for a second income. Iceland's housing market has been under pressure since the financial crash as many building contractors went out of business and construction ground to a halt. Its total population is around 330,000 with only 123,000 living in the capital of Reykjavik. The market has been put under more pressure due to homes being rented out on sites such as Airbnb and Booking.com, and a rule passed in 2017 means that those renting a home on the site for more than ninety days must obtain a license. It has also resulted in property prices growing in the country by almost twenty per cent in the last twelve months. (16)

There are two apartments which Roxanna has a mortgage on and one which she owns outright. She has always had good tenants who have looked after her properties but she worries about the viability of every new tenant that she takes on board. As a result, she made the decision early on that she would not let to anyone who was on benefits. This had proven to be a successful strategy. That is, until Roxanna met Lindy who was a friend of a friend. Lindy had a toddler and was struggling to find housing with the space she needed even after an eight month search. Not only was there a housing shortage, but whenever she did find a property that she liked, more often than not the owner would not allow tenants on benefits to rent from them.

Roxanna was mortified with the consequences of her actions of barring people on benefits from letting her own apartments. She had made the decision to attract what she thought would be a more reliable and trustworthy client base. She had not realised that she was actually disempowering, mainly single women, from the housing which they needed. Although the proportion of people claiming benefits is very low in comparison to other European countries, those that do claim benefits of some kind are usually women. Not only had market conditions made it difficult for Lindy to find a suitable home, but property owners like Roxanna were adding to the challenge.

Lindy didn't know that Roxanna was guilty of denying benefit claimants a chance to rent her properties. But Roxanna did think hard about what she had learned from her new acquaintance and took the empowering step of supporting women by removing the barrier to renting her accommodations.

Roxanna hadn't realised she was standing in the way of other women but as soon as she did, she gave them an empowering nudge into what she now calls her "woman welcoming portfolio".

Hear From Stephanie Green

Stephanie Green runs her own feminist company called Dauntless Daughters which is based in the UK. She's had an interesting career and now dedicates her time to inspiring girls and women through the art of storytelling at her company. She creates images and stories showing women and girls doing all sorts of bold and amazing things. From women represented as explorers and engineers to skater girls and kick boxers.

At the age of twenty one she was elected as the youngest District Councillor in the UK. By the age of just twenty three she was Circulation Director at an International Publishing House.

After her first child was born she left to open her own studio called Stephanie Green Graphic Design. It gave her more flexibility as well as creative freedom. Stephanie has now been working in that studio for eight years. While growing the business and raising her girls she had her eyes opened to the world of gender discrimination in children's literature, which lead her to create Dauntless Daughters. The company launched on International Women's Day 2016 and took off like a rocket. Her first book which addressed gender discrimination, grew to be a collection of books, posters, science kits and educational resources.

Stephanie said, "Through my work I tell empowering stories to the next generation of women. I have always said that my books are as much for parents as children. When we read bedtime stories to children, adults think and experience those stories too. I have also been involved in women's education by speaking at conferences, leading meet ups and organising round table conferences. Just last week a woman wrote to me to say that my workshop inspired her to start a girls club at her school. I think we can empower other women just by being in the same room and listening. Women's empowerment is about lifting each other up towards the destination of freedom. We cannot all be strong all of the time, but if we can stand in sisterhood we can make progress.

I wish all women would take the responsibility to empower other women through pride in their femininity. When did we let feminine mean vulnerable and weak? How is it that 50% of the globe, those who can bear life, come to be described as the weaker sex?

So I would urge each parent, each teacher and each storyteller to reclaim the word "feminine". You can be sensitive and you can be strong. You can be a mother and be indomitable. If we could stand in power in our femininity and stand together then that would be progress for all women.

When I joined the social media platform Twitter, I had no idea what I was doing and how best to use it. I tagged this group called @WomenEd who are a thirty thousand strong group of teachers, educationalists and feminists. They have been incredible. Hannah Wilson, one of the founders, gave me confidence in my work. The group have invited me to speak, given me use of a school to hold events, and champion Dauntless Daughters where ever they can. This is a true example of sisters lifting each other up; a grass roots community which exists purely to help further equality by women and for women."

Women Have Wombs

Part 6

The Matter of Maternity

Men cannot give birth. But what if they could? If there was as much chance of a man getting pregnant as a woman when sexual intercourse occurs then would men have a different appetite for sex? Or if it were a given that men would give birth to boys and women would give birth to girls would there be more childless families?

I suspected that the answer to these questions would be a resounding, "Yes". If men had to face more of the responsibility, consequences, and pain of childbirth then I am pretty sure that most wouldn't want children and those that did would most likely think that one child was enough.

I casually tested the question out on a group of thirty of my male colleagues. The body language from those I questioned was revealingly animated as their facial muscles appeared to go in to spasm when they contemplated the question and its hypothetical implications. I was happy to be proven wrong by two of the men in the group who said that nothing would stop them from wanting children and if nature had given them the necessary biology they would not be put off by the pain. The remaining twenty eight men, however, had a very different response. They were very clear that they would not have had children if the task of childbirth had been theirs. Some were cheeky enough to say that women were good at forgetting pain and others were sheepish when asked why they were happy for their partners to experience trauma when they would not be willing to go through the same thing themselves if it were an option.

The matter of maternity gives rise to many questions, issues and opportunities to do with the gender equality debate. Consider the following:

- Perceptions of pregnant female colleagues in the workplace.
- Perceptions of career potential for women of child bearing age.
- The impact on teams when a member takes maternity leave.
- The impact on workload when parents need to work flexibly for childcare reasons.
- The perception of female colleagues when they take multiple maternity absences in quick succession.
- The salary increases a woman misses out on when she's on maternity leave and which she consequently pays for during the rest of her life.
- Women being perceived as the primary child carers as the social norm.
- The male's job taking priority over the female's when a couple are faced with an unexpected childcare issue.
- The emotional and physical impact on females who are both the primary child carer and essential salary earner.
- The implications of paid and unpaid work.

In The Problem with Privilege we saw that a number of women in China had taken on the approach of pushing their careers forwards through not disturbing the men with domestic duties. That is, women changed their situation and themselves, whilst not expecting men to change theirs. The hiring in of low paid female domestic staff does exactly this; it both crystallises and symbolises that the concept of motherhood and housework is primarily the realm of females.

Many issues are involved in the social, economic and political agenda of family. If gender equality through mutual empowerment is a goal, and traditional gender differences are either amplified in the cause of authenticity or diluted down as methodology for equality then how is the care of children to be managed, be that socially, economically or politically?

Public policy and legal provisions can certainly play a part in promoting change towards the desired goal of gender equality. Familial structures which exist in any given society at a point in time are the result of social, economic, political and cultural developments. All societies have an ideal family structure which is held as the norm and that norm has both a direct and indirect effect on gender expectations and gender equality. The family is never an isolated structure, but rather it is part of wider societal processes. Families are intrinsically linked to the labour market and the organisation of social and gendered networks.

Men haven't taken on childcare in anything like the numbers we've been lead to believe from the media in recent years. All you need to do is think about parents in your own network and it crystallises that men are still the minority when it comes to being chief child carer. There is no doubt that worldwide women's participation within the work force has increased year on year over the last century with exceptions in countries such as Afghanistan where political issues have slowed down women's employment opportunities.[5]   Despite many families adopting the dual bread-winner model, it would seem that the result has been only a partial power spread for women across the work place, the home and political life. Women work much more often than men in part time jobs in developed countries. In the main this part time work is to allow the flexibility to provide child care.

A significant step towards a gender equal world is the replacement of the patriarchal family through recognition and promotion of the paternal role in child care. Active state intervention is required to achieve lasting change alongside strong educational campaigns. Responsibility for childcare begins even before birth and during the crucial period after a child is born. Providing paid paternity leave is not just an issue of income, it signifies the extent to which the role of fathers as child carers is valued in any given society.   According to data analysis released by UNICEF, the United Nations children's agency, almost two thirds of the world's children under the age of twelve months (that's nearly ninety million) live in countries where fathers are not entitled by law to take paid paternity leave.[17] In these countries, the policy to pay or not is typically decided by employers.

It shocked me to find that the United States is one of eight countries where there is no state intervention guaranteeing paid parental leave for either mothers or fathers.   The USA lags behind a number of low income countries where paid paternity leave is offered as well as maternity leave. For example, Tajikistan, Uzbekistan and Mongolia offer more than fourteen weeks of paid leave for fathers. At the time of writing, there are ninety two countries where there is no national policy for paid paternity leave. [18]

To achieve an active culture of gender equality both in the workplace and the home, it's essential for men to have an equal chance to be there with their newborn babies.   As with so many gender equality laws, Sweden got there before much of the rest of the developing world, introducing paid paternity leave options from 1974.   Swedish income taxes are high but a large share goes into providing a work life balance within society for both males and females.

The benefits of paternity leave are significant. Firstly, fathers who use this leave are more likely to take an active role in child care responsibilities. I had conversations with more than one hundred fathers in Iceland who had taken paternity leave; they were more likely to feed, dress and bathe their child long after the period of leave had ended. Furthermore, parents of both genders who took time off at birth were almost a third more likely to read books with their toddlers than those who hadn't.   Secondly , this early interaction has longer term benefits for a child's learning abilities.   However, this tends to benefit children whose parents come from more financially advantaged backgrounds. Most paternity leave tends to be short and not fully paid so wealthier fathers are more likely to take the time off.   Thirdly, and perhaps most importantly for the purpose of this book, paternity leave is good for women's careers. When childcare responsibilities fall exclusively on the mother, the effect is to depress women's wages. Time out of the work force deprives them of pay rises, experience and promotions. When men share more of the childcare responsibility, the effect on women's careers is lessened.

For years the priority for women's rights campaigners has been to increase the provision of maternity leave. These days, more governments are starting to believe that the best way to improve women's career prospects is instead to turn to fathers to take on more of the child care responsibility. In Sweden, Norway and Iceland, where new parents are paid eighty to one hundred per cent of their usual incomes while on leave, between eighty five per cent and ninety per cent of fathers take up these rights. In Britain, on average one per cent of men take more than three weeks of paternity leave as part of their shared parental leave opportunity.[19] However, Britain is only three years in to the concept of shared leave and there are still cultural changes which are required to increase this number.

The British system gives mothers all the leave and then allows them to hand over some of their entitlement to fathers. So the very question, "Why don't fathers take up the entitlement," is flawed. I spoke to a number of parents-to-be in the UK about whether the fathers in the relationship would be taking any more than the statutory paternity leave and the answer from every couple I spoke to was a resounding "No".

However, every male in the couples I spoke to said that they were happy to take more leave to care for their new born; the females in the relationship did not want to lessen their own leave in order to allow the father to have this opportunity. It was very clear from the women I spoke to that they would be going through the pain of child birth, and so they would not be giving up any of the "rest time" of maternity that followed. This means that if fathers were to be offered the same leave as mothers (allowing parents to choose absolutely freely on an equal basis) then fathers would take leave in bigger numbers. It really is that simple as demonstrated by Iceland, Sweden and Denmark.

Societies also won't be able to eliminate the gender pay gap without making it more culturally acceptable for fathers to do more for their children on a consistent basis. Fortunately, there is a tried and tested way of achieving this: to provide a significant chunk of "use it or lose it" leave reserved for new fathers. Several countries have introduced this to great effect. For example, in Iceland, mothers and fathers get three months of leave each, paid at eighty per cent of average earnings, with a further three months to be allocated between them. The vast majority of Icelandic fathers take their leave. It is therefore little wonder that Iceland has topped the global gender rankings for the last nine years.[20]

Women's surprise weapon in the fight for equality could be pitching for better workplace benefits for fathers. We have to make it acceptable for men to embrace an approach to work and home balance that's closer to that taken by women. Otherwise it is likely that gender equality and fair pay will remain a distant dream.

As women we have a responsibility to support mothers who choose (with their partners) to share parental leave. Rolling our eyes and saying, "Well I wouldn't be doing that!" is completely unhelpful. As female leaders, when a male colleague in your team asks for flexible childcare options, you'll be doing another woman a great favour by accommodating the request where it is feasible. We also have a big responsibility to our female colleagues when they return from maternity leave. Too often, women are expected to prove themselves again when they re-enter the workplace as if "baby brain" means that they have to retrain. This period of proving ourselves again slows down career growth and is completely unnecessary. Yes, women may need a few weeks of re-orientation to catch up with things which have changed, but we should not have to prove ourselves in roles we have already been successful in; and neither should we expect our female peers in wider society to prove themselves again either.

For women to get more leadership positions, one of the things which will help us is to champion for more paternity leave. This is not only because women will not be the default option when it comes to being chief child carer, but that more gender-neutral family leave would disable the expectation by employers that young men will necessarily provide greater returns for training and mentoring than young women. The stigma and risk of childbirth and associated parental leave is currently sat firmly with women, and yet it is men who are able to procreate until they die if they so wish.

Men must take on their fair and equal share of child care. As women we can help to create a work culture which encourages parents of either gender to make time for their families. We need to enable and amplify the changes for the betterment of gender equality.

For Each Other: Toolkit Action 8

Remember that giving birth isn't easy

The sad social reality of our current times is that women have to work harder and shine brighter than men to get noticed. Add giving birth into the mix and our working lives are a whole lot more challenging.

Women must be given flexibility in order to progress as one of the things we can't change is that it is women, and not men, who give birth. We must empower women to work from home if this supports them and we must also allow them to re-invent themselves after a break in their career if this is what they wish to do. Ultimately, the flexibility will pay off for both men and women through more gender diverse workplaces across all levels of seniority.

It's also important to remember that the act of giving birth itself is excruciating, not to mention the marathon of pregnancy beforehand. Just because giving birth is commonplace does not mean it is any less painful. Dismissing or sneering at our female peers for pregnancy pain, pregnancy absences from work or pregnancy issues whatsoever means devaluing their personal experience. One of my friends was even told by a midwife that her pushing technique during childbirth was "pathetic".

Give childbirth the respect it deserves. Ensure men are as responsible for childcare through paternity leave legislation and cultural expectations. Flexible hours for men benefit both men and women; flexible hours for women benefit both women and men. It is a current reality that men can become biological parents at any point in old age but after menopause women cannot. Therefore, women pose less of an employment flight risk for parenthood reasons than men if parental responsibilities are equally shared. Put simply, men have more time to become parents and yet women are currently penalised with the maternity leave eye rolls.

Hear from Deborah Rodriguez

Deborah is an author, hairdresser and hypnotist who lives in Mexico. She became a hairdresser at the age of seventeen, working in her mother's salon while she also studied music and criminal justice. Her education gained her a job as a Corrections Officer in a medium security men's prison, all whilst she cut hair on a part-time basis.

She said, *"Spending my days with a bunch of felons didn't suit me well, and my kids kept telling their teachers that their mum couldn't come meet with them because she was in prison."*

So after her brief career in the criminal justice system, she went back to working as a hairdresser in the family salon. Then, in 2002 she made the courageous decision to go to Afghanistan with a medical team and moved her life there soon after in order to co-found the Kabul Beauty School and The Cabul Cafe. While working in Kabul she began her career as an author and to date has penned six highly acclaimed books. In 2009 she moved to Mazatlan in Mexico where she continues to write, cut hair, run a spa and work in hypnotherapy. Deborah has many accomplishments, but her proudest and most rewarding are establishing the Kabul Beauty School and Coffee House, in large part because of how many women's lives were transformed as a result.

On the subject of women's empowerment Deborah generously shared some key moments from her life:

"As a hairdresser you are constantly working with people to help them find both their inner and outer beauty. Feeling good about yourself and the way you look is always very empowering, even if it's just for that one moment. Being raised in a beauty salon I was always taught that our job as hairdressers was so important to the world. That is the reason that I decided to work with the Afghan women teaching them hairdressing.

I know what it feels like to be in a bad and abusive marriage. I also know that it was because of my skills as a hairdresser, and the financial independence it gave me, that I managed to pull myself out of that toxic situation. Hairdressing is so much more than doing hair. I am proud to say that over two hundred Afghan women graduated from the Kabul Beauty School, and are today using their skills to financially help their families.

When I arrived in Mexico, it was really hard for me to sit and do nothing but drink margaritas on the beach. Don't get me wrong, I love a good margarita, but it began to get boring. I needed to be doing more. That is when I opened the spa and began to train and employ local women. Later, I started the non profit called Oasis Rescue, providing scholarships to beauty school for disadvantaged girls.

On a side note, there was a time in my son Noah's life when he was trying to figure things out and, honestly wasn't being very successful at it. I told him to go to beauty school. He wasn't that thrilled about it, but went anyway. Everyone but myself thought this was all a waste of time and money. He was terrible at *doing hair. Who knew that, fifteen years later, he would be in Mazatlán, with four kids and an amazing wife, successfully running our spa on the beach?*

I believe female empowerment all starts with the mother. A mother needs to educate her sons on how to treat and respect women and girls. A mother needs to show her daughters what a strong woman looks like and sounds like and acts like. What a different world we would live in if all mothers did this one important thing. Another way I am empowering women is with the books I write. I want to always write books that entertain and educate, along with encouraging those dealing with issues of their own. My stories tend to feature strong female characters with diverse backgrounds, yet who, in a way, face the same kinds of challenges we all do. The thought is that if the characters are relatable, they might also be inspiring.

My newest endeavour is becoming a hypnotherapist. I'm really enjoying learning hypnosis. Working with women who have left toxic relationships and helping them build who they want to be, to stop that old pattern from happening all over again. It's such a powerful moment when they can literally toss out the negative stuff and focus on all the wonderful things about themselves. Just the difference in the way they walk and hold their body when they leave the office; you can see the transformation has started and the shift is happening."

To Deborah, women's empowerment means freedom. Financial freedom, domestic freedom, and the freedom to accept herself for who she is.

"If you look at the situations of women on a global level," she says, "I would have to say that education, or the lack of education, is one huge issue. I understand culture and religion, but I don't understand denying a female the right to make personal choices, including the opportunity to go to school. Right now, I am horrified to witness what's happening in my own country of the United States. The blatant disregard for women and the dismissal of their voices.

My advice to women on living a happy, successful and empowered life is to love yourself, forgive yourself, work on getting rid of the junk and the people (if you need to) that are less than positive in your life. While training as a hypnotherapist, I learned that the power of our words runs deep and penetrates our subconscious on a level that we are often not aware of. Be careful of the words you say to yourself and others, and especially be careful of the words you speak to children. Those words can stick with them forever, and not always in a positive way.

I am in a phase in my life when I just don't want to be around people that have negative talk. I am done with that. I am also working every day at changing my self talk. We all have to find our path to empowerment, and it can be very different for everyone. But today, right at this moment, I am focussed on the words in my head, and the words that surround me, my clients in the salon, my children, and my grandchildren." [21]

Language Matters

Part 7

The King is a Woman

James De La Vega is a Puerto Rican street artist who decorates streets in aphorisms such as, "Sometimes the King is a Woman".[22] His street art has, on occasion, been seen as vandalism for its disruptive content and nature.

Whatever your personal views on street art, graffiti and vandalism, it seems that there needs to be some disruption to our languages in order for women to empower women. The subjugation of women is hard wired in to the English language and culture. Take the "United Kingdom" for example. As I write, it is indeed a Kingdom by noun but is actually a Queendom by adjective. It is a nation with a female monarch: a Queen. Therefore, from a gender equality perspective I would argue that it is the "United Queendom" although I have never heard it referred to as that.

The term "Kingdom" in the case of the UK is used to denote that it is a sovereign state and that sovereign may indeed be male or female. Conversely, in Saudi Arabia, a ruling monarch can only be succeeded by a male member of the royal family. The issue of succession is handled by what is known as the Allegiance Council and it is possible for the Council to consider a female monarch should it so wish. However, there have been no reported instances of females being considered as ruling Monarch. In the Kingdom of Saudi Arabia, the King has never (yet) been a woman. Therefore, I assert that in the case of Saudi, the term Kingdom is an accurate reflection of the current state, but in the case of the United Kingdom, it is inaccurate and upholds a patriarchal linguistic structure which subjugates the position of women in current society.

The issue of gender within language has long been debated in the context of job titles. In recent years, the title of Chairman has been adopted by female Chairs who have preferred to use the term as their own feminist statement instead of, Chairwoman or Chair. The majority of dictionaries, language guides and terms of reference refer to Chairman as gender neutral. However, to remove historical bias, it must be questioned why the term Chair is not universally adopted as yet. There is still wide reference to actors and actresses, mayors and mayoresses, waiters and waitresses. Gender specific job titles abound, but then so do gender neutral titles such as doctor, teacher, lawyer, lecturer and Member of Parliament to highlight just a few. Whether they are gendered or not, job titles carry a significant amount of power in conveying their owner's status within a company and even within society.

Add gender to the whole job title debate and it suddenly becomes even more complex and significant to the concept of power. The UK jobs marketplace is highly competitive, as it is in many countries and therefore job titles can become a career advancement tool to signify status, experience and power within a company. So much so that, sixty four per cent of the people I interviewed said that they would view a title rise as satisfying as a pay rise, mainly because of its longer term career perception equity. For example, "Senior Accountant" was seen as a title rise from "Accountant" by one of my interviewees.

The encouraging news is that within not much more than twenty years or so, policemen and policewomen have become more commonly known as police officers, firemen are now firefighters and male nurses are generally referred to as nurses. In all these cases, language reflects the fact that jobs once largely the preserve of one sex are now increasingly filled by either.

There is also a trend of taking male power head on with an overt display of female power. Take for instance, the huge trend on Instagram and Twitter for women to talk about being a #bosswoman, #girlboss, #sheboss, #womankind and #leadinglady. Of course the terms boss, humankind and leader are gender neutral and readily available to use as part of our everyday vocabulary for both women and men. But the feminisation of historically male terms adds direct assertion to the cause of women empowering women. When a woman says that another woman is a #BossWoman she not only is recognising the relative power of that woman, but also the earned social power relative to the term "Boss" which women have long fought hard for. It is an equality battle that is not yet fully won in the workplace and therefore the feminisation of job titles shows that women are winning new ground, as women and for women, and not necessarily how bosses of decades past would have done. These new titles scream out that there's a new boss in town, and this boss is proudly a woman.

Language matters. There are very few languages, if any, which have no gender bias. Language defines the limits of our thinking, our imagination and our future vision. It was once a radical proposition for women to retain their own names and titles after marriage. My mother kept what is still referred to as her maiden surname. I remember thinking as a child that I was adopted as my surname was different to both my father's and mother's. I later found out that this was partly because my parents couldn't agree on whose surname I should be given and partly because they liked what they gave me as both my first and second name. When I asked my mother why she had a different surname to my father (this was very unusual in 1980s Britain) she said that she had been a Yasmeen all her life and that she didn't want to lose her personal identity and personal history just because she was married. It was a feminist statement well made.

I also had a teacher at school who was seen as wild and revolutionary. Despite having never been married she called herself "Ms" which was as revolutionary then as the gender neutral "Mx" is now. My teacher didn't want the first thing people knew about her to be whether or not she was married. That seemed like good sense to me. Why would a woman want to go around with a label that described she was in a relationship with someone just because it was a societal norm? That didn't seem gender equal at all.

I am so very proud of my mother for the strong and clear feminist choice she made to retain her own surname and her own identity. Her decision and the communication of that decision to me made a huge impression on my consciousness of gender equality. I am proud of my mother for being her own person first and it emboldened me in to realising that I could be too. My relationship, or lack of a relationship with a man, did not have to be the core of my identity at any point in my life. Suffragettes had to fight to make that concept possible but I grew up with that enablement, in large part because of a conscious act of linguistic activism by my mother and one of my senior school teachers. Those acts consciously enabled me to make my own micro activist statements.

I was that girl who bought Lynx deodorant (a brand aimed at men) for my first senior school Physical Education class. It was because it was aimed at men that I knew I had to buy it; I didn't want to be barred from a product because of my gender. I was also that girl who was too uncomfortable to sing patriarchal hymns in school. At least once a fortnight in morning assembly we would collectively sing:

"When a knight won his spurs,
In the stories of old,
He was gentle and brave,
He was gallant and bold,
With a shield on his arm and a lance in his hand,
For God and for valour he rode through the land."

I couldn't understand why the knight was always male; surely a woman could also be gentle and brave, gallant and bold. I would sing along with everyone else, but on the word "he" I would always mime "she" instead. I mimed it so that I wouldn't get reprimanded by the teachers, and my classmates could never understand why I smelled like a fragrant man (Lynx Java and Lynx Africa if you must know) who refused to sing about a male knight. But I knew that in history there probably was a female knight, and if there wasn't then I would imagine that the knight was me. We can only become what we can articulate and we can only articulate what we can imagine and I could certainly imagine being that knight.

That's why language matters to our lives; that's why little changes in grammar and vocabulary and branding can affect the entire architecture of our imagination and our future vision. It turned out that I took my little acts of gender rebellion perhaps too far. I became that girl who wore men's shirts to make a feminist statement. I pretended that I hated dolls because I thought that my gender dictated that I was expected to like them. At the age of ten, I even spent my precious pocket money on specialist magazines about aeroplanes and helicopters because I thought that it was a way of addressing gender inequality. The truth is that I found helicopters boring and I looked damn ugly in big baggy men's shirts but no-one knew I disliked my mannish statements except me. It wasn't until I left senior school that I realised that being a feminist was about being proudly me; it wasn't about being a male version of me. Fast forward a couple of decades and I'm now a designer of women's heels. I design heels that I know women will love, not heels that men will love for women to wear, or which women wear for men to love looking at whilst they wear them.

I have learned that empowering women is about enabling others to confidently be their own best self. Not a replica of a perceived male self; not a replica of another female self; but a confident and happy in themselves kind of self. Attempts at women's emancipation which are focused on assimilation to the male norm cannot be considered emancipatory.

In an equal world the knight can be a woman if she so wants. She may choose to serve her queendom and work hard to actively and consciously support womankind. That's not to say that gender neutral language and gender inclusive language is not a way forward. It is to say that conscious empowerment, often through a serious wo/manipulation of language can be very empowering on a local, societal, national and even global level.

Words can bring us together or they can tear us apart.

For Each Other: Toolkit Action 9

Notice and call out gendered ruthlessness

When you, or women around you, are confronted with challenge and criticism consider whether this is fair challenge or whether it is gendered ruthlessness. For example, the media have a tendency to use more demeaning and even demonising language when it comes to female ministers compared to male ministers.

A scan of the comments on a range of blogs also evidences that public opinion is often more ruthless towards women. Both by women against women and by men against women. It is sad how far people have actually gone when writing derogatory comments online about female Members of Parliament in particular.

Here are some tweets which appeared about female Members of Parliament during the Brexit Referendum in the UK:

"Bitch. What does that cunt know? She's just good for a fuck."

"She's just a bloody idiot. What does she know about politics?"

"She hasn't got any kids. How can she really give a fuck about our future without any sprogs of her own."

Gendered hostility in the UK is commonplace. Take the media harassment against Dianne Abbott, MP in

2017, when all she was doing was fighting with determination for important issues. She was hounded by the press for getting her numbers wrong (a slip of the tongue which many male politicians have also experienced but not been hounded for). She stuttered with nerves at times and was penalised for being a woman, black and overweight. It was so bad that Dianne actually had to take time off work to repair her health.

Take also the case of Prime Minister Theresa May; hounded by the press for delivering a poor speech because of a cough she struggled to control and a man who ran up to her to hand her a P45 (a document which signals the end of a given employment). She could neither control her cough nor the man who sabotaged her speech by running on stage with the aforementioned document, yet she was harassed because of these two things. At the Conservative Party Conference in 2018 a year later, Theresa was congratulated by almost every newspaper in the queendom for not coughing. The content of her speech and her strategy for Brexit came second place to those who reported on it.

Point made.

For Each Other: Toolkit Action 10

Mind your language

"She wears the trousers" and other such exclamations just aren't helpful in the gender struggle. Statements like this may be made as an acknowledgement of strength or awe but they serve to embed women into the structures of society as secondary to men. It's so easy to use cliches to express ourselves that although we don't mean any gender harm through our language the result is often that we are causing long term empowerment damage.

Next time the word, "bitch" or "cow" comes to mind, stop and think, and then find some other form of words which is fairer to our own sex.

Unconscious sexism is not okay.

Each Other: Toolkit Action 11

Mind their language

It's all too easy to passively wince when someone else uses disempowering language in everyday situations. Like the waiter (male or female) who passes you the menus with a friendly but condescending, "Here you go girls" even though it's obvious that you're a woman and not a girl. Like your boss (male or female) who exclaims, "That's my girl" when you slam dunk a presentation. Like your male colleagues who roll their eyes and display negative body language when a new maternity leave is announced. Like the manager who says that something has gone "tits up" in a meeting.

If you act like you don't mind by allowing sexist language and sexist body language to pass by without comment or challenge, then this language will continue and in time becomes even more normalised.

When you mind, make sure that people know.

Hear from Sarah

Sarah is a single parent to two young daughters and lives in Kensington in the UK. Like so many parents she is often baffled, frustrated and amused by some of the things that her children say. One day on the walk home from school, six year old Gemma and five year old Georgia began to squabble.

Georgia was angry with how much Gemma was worrying about being taunted by another girl in class that morning. Georgia wasn't in the same class and so didn't hear the taunts first hand but thought that Gemma was being too sensitive and should have stuck up for herself.

"You need to grow a pair!" declared Georgia.
"Grow a pair of what?" replied Gemma.
"I don't know," said Georgia, "but you need to grow some."

At first Sarah laughed from the depths of her belly when she heard this unsisterly exchange. Sexist language was everywhere right now, from daytime television to coffee shop conversations, and it was difficult to keep the children away from it. The problem for Sarah was how to deal with it in an age appropriate and helpful way.

She decided to take the opportunity to explain to her girls why she didn't consider the language accurate, fair, or acceptable. "It's a tricky topic but had to be dealt with in the moment," said Sarah. It was an uncomfortable conversation but she proceeded to tell

Georgia and Gemma that if a person does not already have a pair (of testes), then they cannot grow a pair and that this is no bad thing because not everyone needs to have them.

"If we can't grow a pair of testes Mummy, then can we still be besties?"

The girls chuckled at the rhyme. The conversation continued and it weighed heavily on Sarah that it was chatter like this that would influence the girls' views of masculinity and femininity way in to the future.

Handled carefully, Sarah hoped that it was an exchange of words which the girls would recall as a key life lesson in sexist language for years to come.

Exploring Icelandic Feminism

Part 8

Fire, Females and Ice

Iceland has long been deemed the best place in the world to be a woman. For the past nine years, the country has topped the World Economic Forum's gender equality index. The UK comes in at 15th.[5] In Iceland men get at least three months paternity leave, and ninety per cent of them take it.[20] This gives them time to become comfortable with child-rearing, encouraging them to share the workload with their partners. Women in Iceland are highly educated, a high percentage hold managerial positions and they don't give up their careers to have children: they do both alongside their partners.[19] At the end of 2017 Iceland got its second female Prime Minister, a forty one year old with three young sons.

In the UK, 2018 marks one hundred years when some, but not all, women were granted the right to vote. There have been many celebrations to mark the event. But perhaps to commemorate this centenary, women in the UK should have demanded a change in legislation to mirror Iceland.

At the start of 2018, Iceland became the first country in the world to make companies prove that they are not paying women less than men for the same work. Employers are floundering to comply with the new rules to avoid fines. Companies and government agencies with more than twenty five employees must obtain government certification of their equal pay policies. It is a much needed piece of legislation, as even in Iceland, there is a marked gender pay gap. Legally enforcing equal pay for the genders shows how seriously the country is taking the gender pay gap and something which every country should put in to place.

On 24th October 1975, the women of Iceland refused to show up for work.[23] They refused to cook, clean or look after their children. Basically, they went on strike. That day, the supermarkets in Iceland allegedly ran out of sausages (a key convenience food in the country at the time) albeit the sausage rush may be a little bit of local folklore. By going on strike the women of Iceland were demanding to be noticed. They were calling on men to respect their work and demanding equal pay. It didn't matter whether the women were in paid employment or whether they spent most of their time running the home and looking after children. Paid or unpaid they decided to strike in their masses.

It is no exaggeration to say that the country came to a halt, wild panic ensued, and then lasting change came. A change that ensured women were more equal than they had been before. However, as we've established, more equal is just not enough. As recently as 2016 another mass protest was held. Despite being one of the best countries in the world for gender equality, women still earn on average fourteen to eighteen per cent less than their male counterparts.[23] According to Icelandic Unions and Women's Organisations, this means that in every eight hour working day women are essentially working without pay from 2.38pm.

And so at 2.38pm on a bright and cold afternoon in 2016 in the country's capital, Reykjavik, thousands of women again gathered in Central Austurvöllur Square when they left the offices, shops, factories, and schools where they were supposed to be working. Similar but smaller protests are thought to have taken place around the country. It was the kind of activism I was hoping to see in the UK in my opening chapter. The difference in Iceland was the propensity for women to act on gender issues, both individually and collectively, something which we are far behind on in Britain. Women's collective action has been key in the Nordic countries and is especially evidenced in Iceland.

It is widely reported that on the strike day of 1975, ninety per cent of women did not work.[23] Some had to make the idea of a strike more palatable for their employers, and in order to avoid being dismissed or penalised, took the day as a "day of rest" instead; but nevertheless the majority of Iceland's women did not attend work or do any kind of domestic work. I spoke to Hekla, a woman who worked in a cafe just outside the city centre in a place called Laugardalaur during the year of the strike. At the time, she had decided to be one of the minority of women who did not take the day off. She does not regret her decision as she felt that she would have been putting her job at risk at the time; a job she needed to feed her two young children. However, she said that the strike did make her think hard about why her male colleagues were paid more than her and made her more conscious over the years about gender inequality.

Hekla has two daughters who both left work at 2.38pm during the 2016 strike. Her growing equality consciousness had a huge impact on how she brought up her daughters, despite being one of the non-activists during her years of employment. She professes how proud she is of their decision to stand tall with other women activists in Reykjavik.

One year after the 1975 strike, Iceland formed its Gender Equality Council and passed the Gender Equality Act against discrimination in the workplace[24]. Iceland's day of activism led to lasting action. In the land of ice, it was female fire and gumption which achieved meaningful change. Women's movements around the world have often been unable to translate their social mobilisation into political power. Not so in Iceland.

At this point, it would be remiss of me not to mention the issues of intersection and the challenges which Iceland and other Nordic countries have had with this. Women have certainly appeared to make the most progress in terms of gender opportunity within Nordic contexts, but my conversations with lecturers, politicians and journalists in the country signal that this progress is only for the inclusion of the dominant ethnicity women. They also agree that although Iceland's women have been winning in translating social action in to political change, they then struggle to translate political power in to economic power. This is why we still see the gender pay gap in Iceland, and also why we see women at the more pigmented scale of the colour spectrum with an ever bigger gap between themselves and their less pigmented female counterparts.

It is estimated by Icelandic scholars that women have eighty seven per cent equality in Iceland's economy, education, health and politics with women higher in the pigmentation scale having significantly less equality. It may seem like a big number, but eighty seven is still thirteen points short of where it needs to be. The ethnically homogeneous country of Iceland, to its credit, is also home to a number of feminist groups which work on intersectional feminism. For example, there is a network for women of foreign origin living in Iceland called "Women of Multicultural Ethnicity Network" in order to bring about equality for them as women and ethnic minorities. There is also a group called "Taboo" which addresses intersectional issues related to disability activism and there is an organisation called, "Men Take Responsibility" which raises awareness of violence against women and provides services to men wanting to stop physical and verbal assaults.[25]

Ten years ago, in the autumn of 2008, the global economic crisis hit Iceland like an invisible glacier. It was such a dramatic economic disaster that Iceland's three banks collapsed and had to be nationalised, its currency lost half of its value, and the average gross national income plummeted. One lecturer at the university told me that they remember people taking home half of the pay that they had received the year before. Iceland's economy returned to its pre-crisis strength during 2014, ahead of other countries that had a similar crisis. The economy's new revenue was supported by the technology and tourism industries as well as the power of female intervention.

Notably, the collapse of Iceland's government had led to a significant intake of not just women, but feminist women, in to formal institutions of power. The growth of feminist women in charge was felt across various spheres of government, education and the media. In the words of an Icelandic school teacher, "The men had gotten the whole country in to trouble so it was up to the women to get us out. Had we left it to the men we would still be in the frozen economic crisis surrounded by political glaciers. The women stepped in and so we were all able to step out of the economic cold."

Women had indeed played a hugely prominent role, setting up a Women's Emergency Government which was a type of shadow government that trained politicians on the concept of gender budgeting and gender issues. The interim government was also formed by female politicians and it was at this point that Johanna Siguroardottir, who lead the Social Democratic Alliance, and was the longest serving Member of Parliament, became Prime Minister. Her party had a feminist ideology at its core that was crucial to achieving the changes that were to come.[26]

With so much female collective action at a political level, in the distant past, recent past and current day, why then are women still not at parity with men in Iceland today? The women I spoke to across all spheres linked the disparity to informal power networks, or more casually, as gendered social power. In the UK we would call this the Golf Club but in Iceland it is known as the Fishing Club. Male dominance has remained unbroken because of the informal networks where elite men in power are empowering elite men on the fishing boats and beyond. Men still have the leading edge in Iceland because they never really lost their informal power despite the formal changes which came about during the economic crisis. Politics remained a game of invisible networks and so although significant change has been seen, full gender equality is yet to be achieved. However, it cannot be denied that Iceland has a healthy gender ambition and the measuring and reporting of their gender equality progress is certainly continuing to help.[26]

One of the things that Iceland does particularly well is measuring gender statistics. An organisation called Statistics Iceland has published the leaflet "Women and Men in Iceland 2018" in cooperation with the Centre for Gender Equality and The Ministry of Welfare. The leaflet has information on the status of women and men in the community. The numerous tables and graphs can be summarised as follows: [19]

More than half of women aged twenty five to sixty four had tertiary education compared with just over a third of men at the same age in 2017. Around fifty six per cent of women and forty three per cent of men in the capital region had tertiary education, but this measure was forty one per cent of women and twenty per cent of men in other regions. On the other hand thirty nine per cent of men and twenty six per cent of women in the capital region had upper and post-secondary education compared with forty seven per cent of men and twenty nine per cent of women in other regions. The share of people with compulsory education only was roughly twice as high outside the capital region as within it.

In 2017 the labour force participation rate was seventy nine per cent for women and eighty six per cent for men. The unadjusted gender pay gap was sixteen per cent in 2016 but fourteen per cent for full-time employees. Women are now thirty eight per cent of elected members of the Althingi and forty four per cent of local government members but their share in many other positions of influence is lower. Of the eight judges in the Supreme Court one is a woman but women's share among district judges was forty three per cent in 2017. The proportion of women as managers of companies varies by size. For example, it was twenty two per cent in companies with up to forty nine employees but ten per cent where the number was two hundred and fifty or more employees in 2016. The share of women on boards of directors was twenty six per cent to thirty nine per cent by size of company.

Behind every statistic lies a complex social reality. In Iceland, as in every single country of our patriarchal globe, there is considerable need for improvement. Icelanders are rightfully proud of their progressive statistics, but prouder still of the continuing fight for progress and the refusal to accept the government's obstacles. The Icelandic Women's Rights Association has fought for women's rights and gender equality since 1907. They have been members of The International Alliance of Women, since their inception. On October 24th 2018 the IWRA arranged another female walk out, but this time at 2:55 p.m. to reflect the current pay gap. The women of Reykjavik and beyond were encouraged to meet to again protest income inequality, sexual harassment and violence in the workplace. Informal male power networks, such as men's fishing clubs have made it hard for women to gain full power parity with men. So the protests continue.

To understand why "more equal" is just not enough, even in the Icelandic context, then consider this:

- **1975**: Women in Iceland went on strike from work, to demonstrate the importance of women's contribution to society.

- **1985**: Women left work again, to protest income inequality.

- **2005**: The third Icelandic women's strike happened to protest the gender pay gap, at 2:08 p.m.

- **2010**: Women in Iceland went on strike again, this time at 2:25 p.m.

- **2016**: Icelandic women left work at 2.38 p.m on their strike day.

- **2018**: The strike began at 2.55 p.m.

This means that women have gained only half an hour in eleven years, which is less than three minutes per year. If the progress continues at the same pace, Icelandic women won't reach equal pay until 2068. This is clearly unacceptable.

It seems the statistics on women's empowerment in Iceland can look good or they can look bad depending on whether you are an Icelandic man or an Icelandic woman. Women have made notable gains statistically without the progress in truly meaningful representation.[23] Gender power is linked to informal power and to create lasting equality we need to map the entire influence structures across society.

Icelandic models still tend to assume that feminists have to persuade policymakers and the public, through rational arguments, ignoring the power plays and compromises that are posed through informal and established male power networks. [26]

Society's structures must find a way to fairly and openly intersection between male and female networks.

The Wilted Penis

It surprised me that Iceland is home to a museum which, strangely and unnecessarily in my opinion, glorifies the penis beyond it's natural worth. This was an experience which, on a personal basis, I found very unpleasant, in large part because of the unclear purpose of its homage to the specimens on display. However, it would be unfair of me not to mention that there were several groups in the museum who were enjoying looking at the exhibits.

In the town centre of the country's capital, there is a building which is named, "The Icelandic Phallological Museum". This was the busiest building I saw, where women, men, children and even families wandered the exhibit. The museum contains a collection of more than two hundred penis and penile parts belonging to land and sea animals which can be found in Iceland. [27] It includes three specimens from male humans (all wilted beyond recognition when harvested from the bodies) and boasts about being granted legally certified tokens for future specimens from human males.

The whole experience was a strange one. When asked why this museum existed, the said owner's response was, "The answer to that is, why not? Every animal has a penis." I offered that every animal does not have a penis, every male animal does, and asked to genuinely understand the desire behind creating this phallological collection. To which again the answer was, "Why not?" rather than a clear reason why.

I found the museum unnecessary due to the glorification of the pickled male form, at the expense of females. I am confident in calling out the sexism as I saw two representations of females in the items on display. Both were vulgar and demeaning to women, especially one image of a woman being suffocated by a giant penis. The museum claims on its marketing materials (I cannot bear to bring myself to say "literature") to be "scientific" and yet it mocks women a number of times. There are slogans of penis glee around the whole unit; stories of manhoods which have been lost (reverting the ex-penis-owners to a status of so-called womanhood); pickled penises and dried penises. Sadly, there is also an official declaration framed on the wall which asserts that in the museum's opinion:

"Only those who are above average IQ have the mental capacity to appreciate The Icelandic Phallological Museum. According to standards one half of mankind is above the average IQ."

I am not worried about my intelligence after this visit although I am confused as to whether "manhood" in the declaration is referring only to male humans or humankind as a whole including women. I am also left confused about the purpose of the existence of this self professed scientific collection which glorifies the penis and demeans women.[28]

On exploring the town further, my friend and I also came across some souvenir condoms. They were marketed as: "Enjoy our nature: high quality condom from the land of explosions." My friend Kara summed up the product very succinctly. "There are so many world famous natural beauties in this country, and yet sadly there are a few people who can't see past explosions of the man kind. Why ruin world class spectacles with …….. that?"

In defence of Iceland, The Phallological Museum, despite its nationalised name, is a private collection and the tourist condoms were only spotted in two outlets. My thoughts at the end of this particular day were that even in Iceland there is a very long way to go to achieve a true understanding of gender parity. However, my perspective over time is that this museum and the condoms claiming to be on a par with the Northern Lights and gigantic glaciers are examples of individual perversity (or diversity to be kind) as opposed to a national glorification of the man piece. Needless to say that I won't be returning to the museum; but I do not blame Iceland for its existence. That is down to one man and his penile followers.

The Women's House

The Icelandic Women's Rights Association (IWRA) owns Kvennaheimilið Hallveigarstaðir, which is a large building in the centre of Reykjavík. The building is used to house the Embassy of Canada to Iceland, the Embassy of the Faroe Islands, and a suite of meeting rooms to enable a place for females to activate for women's empowerment. Hallveigarstaðir was opened in 1967 and was designed to serve as an intellectual home and refuge for women from all over the country.

IWRA has declared that it will continue to operate until full gender equality is achieved. In recent years, the focus of the work has been increasing women's representation in politics, reducing gender income inequality, increasing the number of women in the police force and the judicial system, lobbying to make gender studies a mandatory subject in secondary schools, and raising awareness about sexual harassment and violence against women. The organisation also actively supports women's culture and encourages the excavation, preservation and celebration of women's history in Iceland.

Importantly, The Icelandic Women's Rights Association is committed to cross-political action. IWRA has hosted annual meetings and talks on gender equality and women's representation in politics, in cooperation with all political parties represented in the country. The group also has a representative on the Gender Equality Council of Iceland and is a founding member of the Icelandic Human Rights Centre. IWRA actively cooperates with partner organisations in the Nordic and Baltic states, and has been a member of the International Alliance of Women (IAW) since 1907.

The goal of a women's centre (or house) arose soon after women in Iceland gained the vote in 1915. At that time, there was a need for a place for women to be able to plan and work for women's issues. The house was opened on Women's Rights Day in Iceland on 19th June 1967, fifty years after the idea was proposed. Notably, the centre was funded by women's groups buying shares in the building; an excellent example of women empowering women. [23]

It was in this symbolic and politically active building that I spent time discussing women's issues with the prolific Executive Manager of IWRA, Brynhildur Heider. She was generous with her insights and explained more about the workings of the Icelandic feminist movement from an active insider's perspective.

My biggest question for Brynhildur was based on the moment I realised why. I wanted to know, how in the strike of 1975, ninety per cent of women were engaged enough to go on strike when in the UK I had struggled to gauge any significant support for action whatsoever — either amongst my peers or beyond. Brynhildur's advice was genius.

She said that a clear goal which everyone can agree on is needed to mobilise women together. In Iceland, this goal is fair pay and affects women at all income levels in society. The strike of 1975 was a catalyst for future strikes, each one becoming easier in its effectiveness of mobilising women to act. As a small country, Icelandic leaders also wanted to do something "to be noticed as a world class nation amongst nations," said Brynhildur, "and the strike was one way of leading the way for women across the globe."

It was explained to me that one way to find the single goal which everyone can unite around is to use existing or future instability to create something new and durable. The financial crash in Iceland made people become activists. It also took a lot of hard work and funds to mobilise women to strike. For the first strike in 1975, volunteers visited every single workplace to engage female employees and ensure that they were prepared to join in with the planned activism. This took a year to complete and a lot of hours of resource which was only available via the goodwill of a number of activists who gave their time freely to the cause. Eighty per cent of Icelanders are members of a union which at times makes it easier to communicate and do collective bargaining.

An element of the effectiveness was also down to calling the strike a "Women's Day Off". The word "strike" politicises the action and can make people nervous, but a "day off" sounds more engaging. However, five strikes later the Women's Day Off is now often perceived as a national holiday and is starting to lose the impetus it once had. For the purposes of the media, the event is called a strike but for engagement purposes with the public, for now, it is still called a day off as this is also inclusive of women who do unpaid work in the home. [29]

The key takeout from my meeting at The Women's House was that as women in the UK (and beyond), we need to be ready to act, just like the Icelanders did. Seizing a moment is so much easier and more effective than creating a moment. For example, The Women's March after Trump's inauguration is likely not to have happened had Trump not been elected. Sexual misdemeanours by the President were called out good and proper. In the UK, this moment could well be Brexit in 2019. Seasoned feminist activists need to be ready to influence, engage and mobilise people. In Iceland, it was the financial crash which made people become activists. It enabled women to take a more active political role, even though it meant cleaning up the issues left behind by the men, which lead to a wealth of new female friendly legislation being passed.

Interestingly, companies with twenty five or more employees are legally required to have a gender equality action plan in place. "To have a plan, someone needs to write the plan," says Brynhildur, "and so this means that feminists are now working from the inside whereas before we were trying to break in from the outside." Gender studies also take place in infant schools but there are a number of campaigns working to ensure that it is mandatory in senior schools as well. At present, Gender is offered as an optional topic to teenagers and it is available in every single school. The biggest benefit to Iceland of increased gender studies has been that it has created an increased number of activists which in turn created more aware citizens. It has also become easier for people to call out sexual harassment. Gender studies has led to better understanding across the population of intersectional issues such as race, age, class and sexuality.

The ultimate advice I received at The Women's House was this:

"The UK women's movement needs to be preparing for its moment now. The suffrage movement demonstrated that the desire and courage is there. It's time to now prepare for a new moment and use the instability of Brexit to create something new and durable and more equal."

Although we have established in prior chapters that more equal is not enough. We do need to start somewhere as long as we acknowledge that an improvement is not a reason to stop pushing for equality. In Iceland, male anti-feminists can be heard saying that, when the varied elements of women's pay are accounted for (such as periods of maternity leave), then the gender pay gap in Iceland is "only eight per cent". If every man in Iceland were to receive an eight per cent pay cut I am pretty sure it would not be seen as "only eight per cent". Besides which, since women are the only sex capable of giving birth, Icelandic feminists are campaigning for equal pay without creative baby bump accounting which hides the real gap, currently at fourteen per cent. Unpaid work, such as giving birth and childcare, is an important factor in the economy, and therefore should be recognised as such.

It's also important to normalise gender equality. The Nordic countries are hugely co-operative and carefully competitive when it comes to gender issues.

Digital collaboration is all well and good, but to gain real momentum, activism needs face to face communication and engagement too. The Nordic governments fund regular women's conferences where women come together across borders to empower, inspire and learn from each other. Progressive legislation needs to be funded so that activists are not left to volunteer through goodwill alone. Secure funding can make or break progression in gender equality.

The last inter-country funded women's Nordic conference led to the making of sixty two overall demands for equality. On the 12-15th of June 2014, thirty thousand people gathered at Nordiskt Forum Malmö (New Action on Women's Rights), to shape strategies to promote gender equality and end discrimination against women. The forum was based on the landmark global agreements of women's rights: the Beijing Platform for Action and the Convention on the Elimination of All Forms of Discrimination against Women (CEDAW).[30]

The forum is the result of two hundred Nordic women's organisations' determination to act. Instead of being silent and waiting for others to act, the collective Nordic women's movement set itself in motion. During Nordiskt Forum, a programme of requirements and recommendations for women's rights and gender equality was adopted. The plan contains clear demands and was handed over to the Nordic governments at the end of the forum. The document is a way of reminding the governments of the commitments made when the progressive

Platform for Action in Beijing was signed.   The demands are centred on:

- The feminist economy
- Women's and girls' bodies
- Women in the workplace
- Ending violence against females
- Environment, climate and sustainable development
- Care work and welfare society
- Peace and security
- Political participation and development
- Gender mainstreaming
- Asylum and migration
- New technologies and media
- Feminism in the Nordic future

The Women's House stands as a powerful and welcoming symbol of empowerment, co-operation and unity.   It shows the determination of the Icelandic people to improve the lives of women and to ultimately work for the betterment of society as a whole.

For Each Other: Toolkit Action 12

Sexual misdemeanours are never ever okay

When you spot it, experience it or witness it then you must speak out. Sexual harassment can be used against men and women, but it is women who are faced with it more often than men. Every study ever undertaken on the topic will endorse this.

Although we know that these misdemeanours are evil it doesn't make it any easier to call them out. However, calling them out is what we must do each and every time. It is never easy but we owe it to ourselves, our gender and humankind as a whole to make sure that we do. It is only through acknowledging evil behaviour as unacceptable that we will make lasting change in society. The #MeToo and #TimeIsNow campaigns specifically engaged women in calling out misogynistic behaviour. They achieved global reach and impact. But it doesn't stop there.

Sexual misdemeanours happen so frequently that they can often be laughed off, ignored or even worse they can oftentimes be endorsed when ignored. It has taken me two decades to become comfortable with having uncomfortable conversations about harassment. In calling it out I have been able to support both men and women who I have seen being victimised and in doing so made it more difficult for other men to consider repeating these evils. For example, there was a male senior manager at work once who had an obsession with lusting after women's feet. So much so that one of my female colleagues said that she was going to come to work wearing a pair of big hairy slippers which said, "Hello" on one foot and the manager's name on the other. The man concerned was very senior so everyone knew who he was and sadly also about his fetish, yet no-one did anything about it except laugh at his foot lusting addiction between themselves. His behaviour made tens of women feel uncomfortable, especially about meeting him on a one to one basis. One day I spotted him so enamoured with a colleague's feet in her peep toe shoes that he didn't hear a word that was said during our stand up huddle meeting. He just stared and stared as if he was watching a microwave meal being cooked; waiting for the ping when he could devour it. I knew it was wrong and I could see my female colleague shifting about from foot to foot whilst everyone giggled. That day, I reported it to my boss (the manager's peer) who took it very seriously and dealt with it appropriately. When I look back on the incident now I wonder why several hundred of my colleagues in head office laughed about the misdemeanours and didn't do anything to stop it. It took me about a year to come forward but it will never take me that long again.

Even today, in 2019, in one of the most developed countries in the world, I have witnessed senior leaders in a number of companies laughing at their colleagues' sexual intimidations and fetishes rather than challenging them. In Iceland this behaviour is much less commonplace.

The more senior the person, the harder it is to put a spotlight on it for fear of career fallout and social stigma as a man hater. If I can give any words of encouragement to the sisterhood it would be this: you can do this. I have spotlighted and raised the alarm about a number of male managers across a number of organisations. All have been more senior than me. I cannot say that the revelations have always been welcomed. People will often squirm and secretly despise you for raising difficult issues. However, I can confidently assert that every time I have been taken seriously and every time at least one of my female colleagues has felt the benefit of my challenge. This may not always be the case but my feelings of female solidarity are stronger than my personal fears now.

Believe me.

It feels really difficult.

It is really difficult.

But you've got this.

For Each Other: Toolkit Action 13

Equality education must start in school and remain on the agenda in all workplaces

Education has been key to acceleration of gender equality.   It is important in primary education, secondary education, tertiary education and in the workplace. Understanding the evolving challenges of gender never stops. Even when we reach equality we will need to continue education at all levels to maintain a gender power equilibrium.

I was lucky enough to be taught Religious Education at school and as a result I am fluent with the beliefs and practices of all of the major faiths. This means that I can interact with people respectfully and do my job serving local communities much better than I would have been able to otherwise. Many people haven't been lucky enough to receive this education and it can seriously impact how they make sense of the world.

For example, one day a customer complaint came in to my department at a retailer I worked for from someone who said that they hated my company's Easter campaign because it did not mention Jesus Christ anywhere. Most of my team thought that this was unfair criticism as a lot of people celebrate Easter as a festival and not a religious event. I reasoned that the team had a valid point, but so did the customer, as Easter was a Christian festival and centred on the resurrection of Christ. "Next you'll be telling me you don't know who Mary Magdalene is," I said in exasperation to my team. "Of course I know" piped up one of my colleagues, "She was in last year's TV series of the 'Bake Off' ". When I had been referring to a woman of historical Christian significance, my colleague thought I was talking about a television show where people bake cakes. Understanding each other's viewpoints has never been so important as it is now.

Although my example above centres on race, it can also be applied to gender.

Education could be a lesson in a classroom at school or a meeting room at work. I recently attended a class on Movember, which was about being extra aware of male cancers during the month of November as part of a national campaign. There are similar campaigns for female cancers, such as Cysters and Breast Cancer Awareness Month.

Being made aware of inequalities means that we are more likely to become citizens who take responsibility for gender equality as well as other justices.

For Each Other: Toolkit Action 14

Disband the Man Club

Encouraging women to take power through their authenticity will only work if the sexist boys club in organisations is disbanded. Women need to make sure not to tolerate this club. Self-perpetuating, non-inclusive behaviour needs to be stamped out. Call out the issues with golfing days; do not accept sexist behaviour and actively voice your desire to be included in team events which are passed off as a "few drinks with the lads".

This does not mean that every male only group or event needs to be disbanded. Men need safe private spaces to chat just as women do. The clubs which need to be challenged are those which perpetuate male informal power over females. That is, what isn't acceptable is male only activity which excludes women from mentoring or sponsorship opportunities.

I sorely regret not challenging the man who said he had nicknamed a candidate he had interviewed as "TT"; I had no idea what he meant until he explained it stood for "teeth and tits". The other men who overheard this found it funny. At the time it was shock which kept me silent. Never again will I tolerate a man speaking like that about another woman. The only way to disband the club is to get comfortable with discomfort and call out the "lads will be lads" behaviour as unacceptable. This comes with risks (for example, people often now think of me as "the woman police") but they are risks which need to be taken.

Exploring Kuwaiti Feminism

Part 9

Discoveries in the Desert

After my illuminating visit to Iceland I made my way to a very different country: Kuwait. Although it ranks highest (thirty seventh) of all Middle Eastern countries on the UNDP gender-related development index, discrimination against women in Kuwait is widespread and has been institutionalised through legislation over a number of decades.[31] Despite this, there are a number of Kuwaiti women who have broken through the gender equality barriers and become highly successful and influential across the Middle East as a whole. It is for this reason that I wanted to complete a visit in the country and find out how some women are breaking through the walls of injustice.

To give a flavour of the inequality faced by women in Kuwait, it is only as recently as 2005 that Kuwaiti women have been allowed to vote and stand for office in parliamentary elections. Earlier attempts by the government to introduce political rights for female citizens had been blocked by Parliament. Spousal rape is not considered a crime in Kuwait. Likewise, Kuwaiti law does not specifically prohibit domestic violence or non-domestic sexual harassment. The inequality faced by Kuwaiti women and immigrant women in the country is huge. Please note that it is commonplace in British society to refer to white people who have emigrated from Europe, Australia or the United States as ex-patriots; whilst people of other colours are referred to as immigrants. For the purposes of this book, I include all colours, races and nationalities who have emigrated to Kuwait as immigrants in order to provide fair and due respect to all. Issues of intersection apply to all people within society and the superior label of ex-patriot is a strong example of this.

Before my visit I discovered that some of the most powerful women in the world are Kuwaitis. Here are just a handful of notable examples from the Forbes 100 Most Powerful Arab Women list from October 2018: [32]

- **Shaikha Al Bahar** is Deputy Group CEO of the National Bank of Kuwait. With assets of more than $74 billion, NBK has consistently received high credit ratings, and was named Best Bank in Kuwait for five consecutive years by the international financial publication Global Finance. Shaikha has more than thirty years of banking experience and also serves as a board member at a number of large businesses.

- **Maha Al Ghunaim** co-founded Global Investment House in 1998; an investment company that went on to become the first Kuwaiti firm to list on the London Stock Exchange. After the financial crisis of 2008, GIH posted heavy debts and was forced to delist. Maha and her team re-engineered the firm, and GIH is back to being profitable, and has $3 billion in assets under her management.

- **Henadi Anwar Al-Saleh** became chair of the board of directors at logistics giant Agility in 2017, when the company split the role of chair and CEO to comply with new governance rules in Kuwait. The company generated $4.8 billion in revenues once she was on board by providing global distribution, warehousing and freight for the pharmaceutical, retail, oil and gas sectors.

- **Rasha Alroumi** is Chair of Kuwait's national carrier and is focused on modernising the Kuwait Airways fleet.

- **Sara Akbar** is an industry leader at Kuwait Oil Company and Kuwait Foreign Petroleum Exploration Company, Sara co-founded Kuwait Energy in 2005. Kuwait Energy is an independent oil and gas company actively engaged in the exploration, appraisal, development and production of hydrocarbons. She was the only female firefighter to participate in her country's Wild Well Killers team, which was formed in 1991 to fight the oil-well fires of Kuwait during the Iraqi invasion.

- **Eaman Al Roudhan** joined Zain Group, a publicly traded mobile telecommunications provider in the Middle East and North Africa, which recorded revenues of $46 million in 2018's first financial quarter. She joined Zain Kuwait in 1998 and together with a team launched the first mobile prepaid service in the country.

A scan of headlines in the British press show that two very inaccurate images of Middle Eastern women are prevalent. The first, is that women have no freedom of choice whatsoever in making key life decisions. The second, that women's subordination is due to Islamic practices rather than the patriarchal, economic and political forces in motion. Muslims are also confused as being of Middle Eastern, African or Asian origin in the vast majority of Western media representations. There are hundreds of thousands of European, British, African, American and Australian Muslims who have white skin and are not confused with oppression, often because the Western media conveniently forgets that white people can also be Muslim.

In Kuwait, women can be found successfully holding roles such as Deans of universities and CEOs of big multi-billion dollar world class businesses. Other than their Kuwaiti nationality, all of the women cited in the Forbes Power List share a strong educational background from universities in Lebanon, the USA and the UK. What is clear from speaking to some of the post holders, is that the roles are occupied mainly by women from the ruling elite and what is referred to as the Kuwaiti "merchant class" who have amassed their fortunes through transformational trade. In these social classes, educated women are not considered so much a threat to male economic dominance and patriarchal tradition, but as an additional way to keep wealth and power within their own social class. When no able elite male is available for a certain position, members of the merchant class are more likely to turn to a female candidate from within their own social group than to a male outsider from the middle classes. This is known as kinship society and it is noticeable how much direct influence this has in social, political and economic spheres. [33]

Also in Kuwait, a high proportion of social, economic and political decisions are made in men's social gatherings called diwaniyas. These are akin to how golf retreats have been used in British culture and perhaps also the use of private gentleman's clubs. In the evenings, men will gather in a diwaniya (a relaxed private lounge in an influential man's house, in the garden of his mansion or in a private club). The most senior male in terms of social standing will act as the chair and men will lounge for hours smoking pipes and working through issues and problems.

The diwaniyas tend to run by invitation only and a key problem that seems never to have been worked through is that of gender equality. Despite several attempts to observe a male diwaniya in action I was never able to secure an invite due to my gender. However, I was allowed to see some of the diwaniya spaces whilst they were not being used. On my tour of these spaces, one of my hosts told me that things are slowly changing and that over the last five years, there have been diwaniyas hosted by women for women and that sometimes women have been allowed to visit a male diwaniya as a guest to discuss a specific topic.

Diwaniyas are where the real politics happen and are frequented by local Kuwaitis as well as male immigrant diplomats and business men who occupy a place in the upper social classes. Domestic house help, cleaners or taxi drivers won't be found at these gatherings as guests, whether they are male or not.

I spoke to a woman called Anan who attended a female diwaniya. She was an active member in years past of The Islamic Care Society whose leaders copied the male format of gatherings and created a safe female space for serious and social discussions. Anan said, "The gatherings happened once a week in the evening and I looked forward to them a lot. They allowed us to talk about the things that are important to us. About our work, our children, our husbands, our problems and even about house work if we wanted to. We openly shared our opinions on all sorts of topics and gave each other meaningful advice. Going to a diwaniya means that I do not feel so alone and helps me in making the big decisions about my life. Men have been the cause of most of my problems and it is my fellow women who have helped me to sort them out."

The diwaniyas are certainly empowering to those who are able to attend and are helping a few women to make some progress in gender equality. However, there is still much change to make to ensure that all sectors of society are represented, enabled and empowered and that meaningful discussions also take place between genders. I was able to attend a female diwaniya and asked the ladies present, "What's it like to be a woman in Kuwait?" The question was met with surprise as most had not considered the topic of feminism, but then after some serious thought there was lots of discussion and comparison to countries such as Saudi Arabia and Qatar where the women knew gender equality was not as strong as in their own country.

In Kuwait, the middle classes rely heavily on civil service jobs in an already seriously overcrowded state bureaucracy. Once a Kuwaiti student graduates, they are guaranteed a paid full time job within a government department. They cannot be sacked from this role no matter what their performance is like; they are guaranteed a well paid job for life. Therefore, the men have more reasons to fear the competition of highly educated women (after decades of struggle women now constitute well over half of the students at Kuwait University) than the men in the more affluent classes. Women in civil service are typically tackled out of the way by males for the higher paying and thus more prestigious and influential positions.[34] Women are still expected to be the primary child carers and therefore huge bias exists in granting men the government roles they want ahead of the women.

This may partly explain why membership in Islamic associations is so popular amongst some modern Kuwaiti women. These organisations offer middle class women a solid single sex platform for acquiring social standing and influence, which has been denied to them by their male counterparts in regular male and female mixed society. [33]

Women's attendance figures at Kuwait University are both impressive and disheartening at the same time. Impressive, in that they are growing year on year. Disheartening in that this is mainly because Kuwaiti men tend to favour studying abroad instead of their own country as it gives them access to higher social prestige and relief from the sweltering desert weather. Women are gaining more access to education, but the men are keeping what they see as the premium educational experiences to themselves and their immediate kinship spheres.

I experienced a flavour of this first hand on a very recent trip to Singapore. I was taking part in an educational visit to a Hindu temple followed by a Hindu meal. One of my dining partners was an American lady who had been hired to tutor a Kuwaiti male student. He was learning about society by travelling the world over five years with his tutor who painstakingly ensured that he was exposed to a variety of different cultures, histories and geographies. The unusual part of the conversation was finding out that the aforementioned male student was not a part of the excursion to the Hindu temple that night. He had stayed behind at the luxury Shangri-La Hotel to soak up what the resort had to offer and his tutor would feed back her findings to him so that he could learn through her experience. She had been selected to carry out this work by the young man's father who approached her after discovering that she had been an experienced private tutor as well as a woman of influence in politics.

I learned that the student's sisters were studying at a University College near home, rather than the luxury resorts their brother was studying from. However, I can also report that I spoke to one Kuwaiti woman who was about to attend Iowa University, USA, to study engineering. Her three older sisters had already graduated from there and studying abroad was something everyone in her family did.

In Kuwait, male privilege and social privilege are clearly at play. With this in mind, how are some Kuwaiti women breaking through the discrimination, and in doing so, breaking through in a big way? That was an answer that I could not find in the diwaniyas so I headed out further into Kuwait City to find out more.

For Each Other: Toolkit Action 15

Understand gender challenges

Societies the world over still put pressure on the female to be the primary carer. There's a lack of diversity training and education that needs to start at a young age. Worldwide there's still the traditional view that men are tougher and better at handling pressure and that women with familial responsibilities might not be up for the top jobs. It comes down to knowing and understanding each gender's challenges. To empower women to gain senior roles it's important that young male professionals are enabled to have a conversation with their bosses about flexible working arrangements so that their partner can go back to work and they can both share the parenting. It's important that we support women to be able to say, "I want to get up to the next level and I also want to be involved in the upbringing of my child."

Women and men have different biologies. We can be different and equal if we take the time and care to think through gender specific challenges.

Hear from Sara Ajlouny

Sara is a Pharmacy student at Jordan University of Science and Technology (JUST) as well as a social and healthcare activist. She was the organiser for the first International Women's Day event at her university which ran under the theme, Celebrating Females in Science. It took place in 2018. She also chairs a Pharmacy Volunteers group which has a majority of female members allowing them to be key decision makers and socially responsible members of the community.

The woman who empowered Sara most was her mother. She said, *"My mother has always been my number one inspiration. I look up to her power, commitment and beauty. What she does every day and who she is, is so fascinating and powerful to behold. She is a devout Muslim, a strong beautiful mother-of-four who believes in the importance of family, womanhood and education.*

My mother is currently a professor at Al-Balqaa Applied University; she is a distinguished published scholar in the field of Education and more recently, has co-founded and co-ordinated a project for young northern Jordanian females to combat unemployment.

For the Jordanian woman, misogyny is an everyday challenge, however, it didn't stop my mother from being a positive and proud feminist. She gave my sister and I the same opportunities and resources she'd given my brothers. She would let us choose our clothes, our friends, our sports, our hobbies, our political views, our favourite music and she would encourage us to make our own responsible decisions. She taught me about religion and art and she taught me how to tend to a family. Naturally, an all-round lady: she oozes class, is a socialite, a great teacher, is active and is an advocate of a healthy lifestyle. She prays five times a day and makes time to listen to the most mundane things I have to say after a long day at work or school. She made sure I never felt different regardless of gender. She instilled qualities of tolerance and respect in us because even when we had markedly different opinions to hers, she accepted us.

Finding females who come from the same background and who also share your troubles has the potential to be a life changing experience. Women's empowerment is a step towards social justice and sustainability. In Islamic culture, a person's ultimate goal in life is to help shape and build the world in to a positive and peaceful place. Marginalising half the population will only serve as an obstacle. That is why women's empowerment is a priority. Women are educators, scientists, mothers and strong decision makers. A critical mass of strong women who empower each other will impact the future positively."

Sara's call to action to women everywhere for a happy and gender equal world is this:

"The world is already so beautiful as it is, but a world that views women as equal to men is more healthy, more peaceful and more sound. Be active mentors for fellow females in your fields of expertise; that is true empowerment." (35)

Shake-Ups

Kuwait began its transformation from desert to urban metropolis in the 1950s when the reigning Sheikh, Abdullah al-Salim Al Sabah, created a welfare state which provided free education, free medical services and housing funds for every single citizen. But he didn't stop there. To ensure rapid and lasting transformation he called in experts from around the world to modernise and urbanise the country. This was when Kuwaiti feminist consciousness began in earnest.

The equity of oil which had enabled the developments meant that Kuwaiti society gained a sudden immense wealth as well as the influx of an immigrant class to support the natively born Kuwaiti population. The rich became even richer and each department of the government was headed by a male member of the ruling family. Statistical tables published by organisations such as UNICEF and the World Health Organisation don't show any measurable poverty in Kuwait. In short, there are no financially stretched Kuwaitis in world poverty terms.

The oil economy did, however, deepen the social divide between the middle classes (those working in government funded jobs such as university lecturers, teachers, administrators and social workers) and the ruling class and merchant class who amassed even more wealth through private companies. Power continued to amalgamate in the upper stratums of Kuwaiti Society placing more social pressure on the women in these classes to take action for enabling gender equality.

The restructuring of the community through the discovery of oil meant that female education started to find a place in the country. The first state school for girls did not open until 1937. During urbanisation, the number of job opportunities opening up were huge and there were not enough men to fill all of the roles, even with an influx of immigrants from around the world. Reluctantly, parents started to allow their girls to attend school to learn basic reading and writing skills which provided an opportunity for female teachers at the predominantly female only schools. Kuwait also wanted to modernise its reputation to the outside world, and it was only by allowing girls to become more visible through education that this would be possible.[33]

Consider the impact of this. It was not until 1952 that secondary school level classes were introduced for girls; and even these took place within the cautious net of primary school buildings. Until 1966 the highest level of education a woman could attain in Kuwait was a secondary school diploma which meant that the highest paying jobs they could take up were as primary school teachers or office workers. Sheikhas and merchant class women attended universities abroad and therefore gained the privilege of competing with men for higher paid titles, roles and responsibilities. This further deepened the class divides.[34]

Outside of the Middle East, it is easy, but not accurate, to believe that Islam has repressed women in majority Islamic countries such as Kuwait. Women who wear the headscarf are often represented as backward, repressed and often even as stupid. What is rarely, if ever, reported is that it is not Islam which has held women back, but men as individuals and as a male collective, and that Islam must in fact be given credit for giving women the tools to emancipate themselves from the strangulation of the established patriarchy. Islam is feminist because it calls for men, as well as women, to dress modestly. It called an end to the practice of female infanticide which was commonplace before Islam's inception. It calls for women to have equal choices and make decisions about their own lives. It is a real shame that influential men who proclaim to follow Islam have interpreted the religion to the benefit of their own gender. It is their influence which has created a culture of sexism and given Islam an unfair reputation.

One of my male colleagues in a major retail company said to me that, "It's only the uneducated women who wear headscarves. I'm not being racist. That's just how it is. I know because I worked in Egypt for years and the women who had a bit of intelligence didn't cover up." Not being racist? Or couldn't see past the headscarf? My conclusion was that my colleague was demonstrating racism and sexism.

In the UK, a record number of anti-muslim attacks and incidents of abuse were reported last year, with women disproportionately targeted by mostly male teenage perpetrators. The British monitoring group called Tell Mama said in its 2017 annual report that it, "Noted a surge in Islamophobic attacks, with 1,201 verified reports submitted in 2017, a rise of twenty six per cent on the year before and the highest number since it began recording incidents." Experts put the rise down to the growth of the far right which has been emboldened by Brexit and the election of President Trump in the United States.

In 2018, the UK's former Foreign Secretary, Boris Johnson, compared Muslim women who wear the burka to "letter boxes". This prompted calls for him to apologise and be expelled from the Conservative Party although neither actions came to fruition. However, a surge in hate crime against women who wear visible head coverings was recorded by Tell Mama following the comments by Boris.

I spoke to a Kuwaiti born lady called Hadiya who had grown up as a teenager in 1970s Kuwait City. She now spends half of her time in Saudi Arabia, and half in Kuwait for work purposes. Her story regarding class differences in Kuwait is intriguing and tells of the empowerment shifts and urban shake-ups which have taken place over time.

Although Kuwait may seem unrelatable for many people, I wanted to include it as it is important that we all see the women who are behind the headscarves. Women who wear a burka, niqab or scarf are actually not that different in their feminist ideals to women who don't wear one. It is not Islam or the burka which has held women back, but male interpretations of how Muslim women should live. It's a very exciting time in Kuwait as things are changing fast. Women are using their faith and rejecting male readings of their religion to emancipate themselves.

In the end, women are all different which is what makes us all the same. There is much we can learn from others with whom we share the same gender, no matter where we are in the world, what faith we have or don't have, what outfits we wear, our level of education or our political allegiances.

Let us stand tall and stand together.

For Each Other: Toolkit Action 16

Spot the men of average talent

As women we need to convince other women that we are as good as men and that we must demand equal space. Always remember, and remind other women, how many men of average talent have reached good positions. In Kuwait this is a lot, and the women are now stepping up and taking the roles they have always deserved.

Use this knowledge to get the gumption to go for things that you want; if you don't then the men certainly will. Women must not be too quiet or too humble; we must believe in ourselves. We are good enough and we should go for the promotions we deserve. Mixed gender groups always function better and deliver stronger results so speak up about the achievements of gender equal groups.

Having gumption can mean many things such as:

- Want that job? Go for it. The worst that can happen is that you don't get it.
- Observed a man take credit for a co-worker's efforts? Amplify her voice and congratulate her on her idea.
- Found out that a male colleague doing the same job as you with the same experience is getting paid more? Ask why and demand for it to be rectified.
- Understand your company's gender pay gap and the actions in place to eliminate it.

- Does your company expect you to lead like a man when you want to lead like a woman? Ask why and demonstrate how you want to lead.

Instigating change is hard and can take many attempts. But that feeling when you achieve it is oh-so-definitely worth it. Do it for yourself and do it for womankind.

Hear from Hadiya

"Kinship barriers were a huge problem at one time. Although it's much better now, power is still held amongst certain families. But not so long ago it was much worse. Money still felt relatively new and those who had it needed to show that they had it in the most opulent ways they could think of.

I should have seen myself as lucky as my family were not poor, but compared to the girls in the upper classes it felt like my sisters and I had very little. Girls of my age in the powerful classes strutted around in top to toe Gucci, used Louis Vuitton holdalls as gym bags and bought expensive cars in bespoke metallic colours for their family chauffeurs to drive them around in. The difference between the classes was this huge gulf which bred resentment amongst myself and my peers.

Before I was born, my mama had taken part in a number of protests against the legislative enforcement of the abaya. She was an administrator for a group of architects and found it cumbersome and ugly as well as something which screamed her gender out loud. A number of protests took place including some college students who burned their abayas. My mama celebrated one scorching day in 1961 when the government finally said that women did not have to wear the abaya to work unless they chose to.

It was the element of choice which caused my mama and her friends to rejoice. Choice is something they sorely lacked at that time.

What might come as a real surprise to you is this. In my late teenage years, alhumdulillah, I yearned to wear the abaya, along with many other women my age. The Islamic abaya became a symbol of unity amongst women of all classes. Islamic dress became a way of showing that we are all equal. Yes, that meant some of the girls my age were wearing Chanel and Prada under their abayas, whilst my friends and I were wearing dresses made by the local seamstress. My abaya became my most loved item of clothing. It became a way of showing public female solidarity across the financial class divide.

I now work in Saudi Arabia and I believe the abaya was a huge part of me securing my role as lead surgeon. People make so many first impressions based on looks whereas the abaya meant that clothing fit, clothing brands and the stigma or prestige which can come from these did not hamper my success in the interview. No-one knows what you're wearing underneath so they have no option but to listen hard to what you are saying. I for one, have a lot to say to those who will listen up."

For Hadiya's abaya to feel empowering she needed the solidarity of her female peers. In her case, the abaya allowed the young women to show a strong solidarity with each other. She wanted freedom and empowerment on her own female terms, and not by copying male norms. The abaya became a symbol of solidarity for her and many others.

He Said, She Said

Female interpretations of Islam, enabled through literacy and religious education by female teachers in schools, opened up a lasting form of empowerment for the women of Kuwait across all classes. It created a way for women to come together despite political differences, financial differences and social differences. Many women found the power to change their lives and those of other women through organising together for Islam. They lobbied, leafleted, spoke and organised protests together. They became a visible and vocal part of history through their prayers by working together rather than being marginal and ineffectual outsiders. Patriarchal interpretations of Islam which suited the menfolk had held them back. Female interpretations helped them to move forwards. (33)

Worshipping God through Islam became the foundation of their lives instead of the previously held foundation and oppression of primarily male rules. The domestic role was no longer a women's only role and how they interpreted their domestic lives began to change.

By becoming feminists in their own right and in their own way, rather than copying Western feminism, Kuwaiti women began to gain a growing feminist consciousness. However, as can be seen in many similar examples worldwide, this consciousness faced severe opposition. For example, during the 1992 National Assembly a motion was put forward to ban Kuwaiti women from travelling abroad without a male chaperone. The motion was not accepted but the very fact it was proposed shows the severe patriarchal structures that Kuwaiti women had to face, and in a huge number of cases are still facing in one form or another today. Male misinterpretations of Islam continue to be fought by Kuwaiti women in 2019.[33]

Through the efforts of the suffrage movement, in 2005, just fourteen years ago, women finally gained the vote in Kuwait. This had been a long and arduous struggle and continues to be to this day. Omaira, a business woman running her own chain of jewellery shops in Kuwait, Oman and Bahrain told me that one of the factors in the slow pace of change was the apathy of a lot of women, many of which are her peers. She told me:

"As a nation we shook up the desert in less than a decade and built this stunning urban landscape that can rival any city in the world. But then when it came to the emancipation of women all of a sudden change became something that happens slowly, stops and sometimes even goes backwards. It's hard getting the buy in of the ruling elite, especially when they are male. It's even harder because it's so very disheartening when women hold themselves and our whole gender back. Lots of women said that they supported the right for females to vote in the late 1990s and early 2000s. But then, when we (active suffragists) asked more women to take part in the movement and demand, fight and keep fighting for equality, we were faced with apathy. Many women wanted the vote but only if other women, or even the men, worked to give this to them. It was only when more of us could rely on each other that we started to see success on the political spectrum. Change is happening but it comes in spurts here. It's sad to think that the likelihood is that even my grandchildren, if I am ever blessed to have any, will probably have to continue the struggle. Women have to help women for men to then help women …. in a meaningful and active way I mean. Inshallah, then things will really start to be shaken up for the better."

From over eighty women whom I spoke to, from across the social, religious, political and economic spectrum, one thing was clear; that what I had learned from The Women's House in Iceland also rang true in Kuwait.

That truth, the enabling truth, is that to gain momentum there needs to be a cause, greater than smashing the patriarchy, for women to unite around in order to make headway in breaking down gendered barriers. In Iceland, the momentum for unification came through a desire for fair pay. In Kuwait, the momentum for unification came through a desire for truth in the interpretation of religion. In both countries, activists were ready to seize moments where women could make headway together. It is these moments which have given rise to a lasting feminist consciousness.

The women I spoke to in both Reykjavik and Kuwait City lamented the apathy of female peers. To take their countries, and consequently the new interconnected world, to a gender equal place, more women need to see, feel and hear much more from each other. This feeling of common concern has also helped to bolster interfaith relationships between Muslim, Christian and Jewish women in particular.

There are numerous Muslim-Christian, Muslim-Jewish, Jewish-Christian, Jewish-Christian-Muslim alliances within Kuwait, the Middle East, Europe, the UK and the United States borne out of practising interfaith kinship. The influx of immigrants in to Kuwait from a number of geographies has also meant that a cross-religious understanding and acceptance is more imperative than ever. Interfaith commonalities across the Abrahamic faiths have brought women together across religions. A key success factor in these alliances has been to highlight the difference between culture and faith, with faith leaders often misrepresenting religious readings in order to endorse the culture which supports their gender. There is also a need to include women from faiths such as Hinduism, Sikhism and Buddhism as well as women of no faith or of no practising faith.

Policies of gender segregation by existing male Kuwaiti leaders have, in a number of areas, actually ended up being positive for the women's rights movement in the country. When women and men complete the Hajj pilgrimage at Islam's holiest meeting place, they do so together at God's house, the Kaaba. There is no segregation when completing the tawaf which is the most sacred act of worship for a Muslim. Despite this, in the Islamic country of Kuwait, under the leadership of male Muslims, segregation has been a big part of setting up daily life in the new urbanised landscape. For example, it is possible to find women only banks, women only restaurants and women only schools. These places of business require women as their operators, their leaders and their customers which means that there are numerous examples of women from conservative patriarchal families who have found contention free employment in places such as women only banks. This has not only given them a valuable role outside of the home, it has helped to elevate their position in society as well as their financial and educational freedom. What this means is that although Islam is feminist as demonstrated by the tawaf amongst many other examples, even patriarchal interpretations have been cleverly used by feminists to engender female gender power and change.

The leading ladies in the Forbes Power List from Kuwait are the embodiment of a new kind of female empowerment. Yes, most have had the privilege of easier access to the best higher education on offer in the world, but they are also aware of the need to use their voices to support womankind as a whole. All of the women have had to work harder, work smarter and work longer under huge amounts of social, familial and political pressure to achieve what they have. As the leading Kuwaiti business women, female politicians and female activists exercise their religious, social, political, legal and human rights, we are seeing them gaining prominence, local and global respect and the ability to lead, and speak for, their entire communities.

It is true of the nature of humankind that there are some people who will be leaders, and some who will be followers. In the struggle for women's equality (and yes, it is and always has been a struggle) as long as there are both engaged leaders and followers I believe that, at some point, we will achieve gender equality. For that equality to take place on a global level, every woman needs to be either a follower or a leader. I am not saying that everyone needs to be a political activist or a modern day suffragette. I am definitely not saying that there is only one kind of feminism; there are thousands of feminisms.

What I am saying is that microcosms of equality are not enough.

To achieve a global gender equilibrium every woman must play her part, even if it is purely in following the lead of others, or in a gentle consciousness of the power of everyday gender activism.

Women of the world: the time has come for us all to unite in our desire to act for our own gender; on behalf of our individual selves, our families, our friends and each other.

For Each Other: Toolkit Action 17

Have the audacity to educate

Educational systems, or even the lack of the systems themselves, are often the biggest challenge to achieving gender parity. It's important for women to have role models, living examples who prove that women can lead, support change and thrive. Both at school and at home women are often expected to behave in a certain way and those biases and expectations come in to play in the workplace. For example, far fewer girls than boys go to engineering school or learn to code. The technology and scientific industries are the ones which will provide the leading jobs of tomorrow. Women need to encourage girls to join these fields because if we don't, the gender imbalance will become even more significant.

We must encourage girls to have the audacity to try things out. To code. To create. To lead. To change.

Feminist Activism

Part 10

Going Guerrilla

Guerilla feminism is about utilising the element of surprise to further the equality of women with men. The term "guerilla" is largely used to refer to non-dominant groups within society trying to counter inequalities through informal activist networks.

There are a number of guerrilla groups and campaigns which are devoted to fighting sexism. These types of campaigns are needed when formal power networks cannot be penetrated in a substantial way.

Guerrilla Girls Talk Back was a campaign comprising of thirty subversive posters put together by an anonymous group of American female artists who wanted to bring attention to sexism and racism. The group's members protected their identities by wearing gorilla masks in public and by borrowing pseudonyms from historical female figures such as Gertrude Stein and Frida Kahlo. Proclaiming themselves the conscience of the art world, in 1985 the Guerrilla Girls began their poster campaign that targeted museums, dealers, curators, and artists who they felt were actively responsible for, or complicit in, the exclusion of women and non-white artists from mainstream exhibitions and publications.

A print of the 1989 poster from the Talk Back campaign asks, "Do women have to be naked to get into the Met. Museum?'" with a reclining naked woman who is wearing a gorilla mask. The image is based on the famous painting by Jean-Auguste-Dominique Ingres from the 1700s entitled Odalisque and Slave and is accompanied by the facts: "less than five per cent of the artists in the Modern Art Sections are women, but eighty five per cent of the nudes are female". The poster was displayed on advertising space on New York's buses, until the bus company cancelled the Guerrilla Girls' lease, allegedly because the image was too suggestive.[37]

The Russian group Pussy Riot is another strong example of guerrilla feminism. It was founded in 2011 in Moscow. The group began to gain momentum after two members, Nadezhda Tolokonnikova and Yekaterina Samutsevich played a recording of Pussy Riot's song "Ubey Seksista" (Kill the Sexist) at a lecture on feminist punk. The Russian media paid close attention to the performances that followed. Later in the same year, Pussy Riot performed on top of a garage next door to the Moscow Detention Centre No. 1, which was holding activists arrested a week earlier at the mass protests against the results of the elections.

At the beginning of 2012, Pussy Riot gained further notoriety after two members were arrested for their Putin Zassa performance at Moscow's Red Square, translating roughly to 'Putin Has Pissed Himself,' the group let off a smoke bomb, and two of the guerrillas were later found guilty of breaking the laws of conducting rallies. A performance by the group against Putin and against patriarchy in the Church lead to international acclaim in 2012. It was called Punk Prayer and resulted in three of the group being jailed, charged with hooliganism motivated by religious hatred. One member was later freed on probation, but the sentences of the other two feminists were upheld, and they were sent to prison. Both women asked to be imprisoned near Moscow in order to be closer to their family; instead, they were sent to labour camps many hundreds of miles away. The harsh sentence attracted international criticism including from Amnesty International.[33]

The Gulabi Gang (Pink Gang) in India is a guerrilla movement which literally fights for the rights of women who have been at the receiving end of gendered violence. Members of the group dress in a uniform of bright pink saris and are armed with bamboo sticks. The gang has over twenty thousand members and was founded by a woman who was assaulted for standing up for the rights of a woman she witnessed being violated by a man. The colour pink was chosen not because of its global female connotations, but because in India it has no political or religious associations.

The gang is committed to addressing   issues of domestic violence, rape and forced marriage and although they are equipped with bamboo sticks they seldom use them. Instead, their actions focus on pressuring police to register and investigate cases, organising protests, raising awareness and providing support to women at risk. However, when the sticks are needed, as no other action is getting the desired response, then the sticks are used. On one occasion, when the group's founder went to the local police station to register a complaint, a policeman attacked her. She retaliated by beating him on the head with her bamboo stick.[37]

Free The Nipple, a recurring protest in Iceland, originally took the streets of Reykjavik by storm in 2015 as women rallied their support behind a teenage student who was bullied for going breast bare[33]. Adda Þóreyjardóttir Smáradóttir, chair of her high school's feminist society, named March 26th 2015, "Free The Nipple Day". She launched the day by posting a bare breast image of herself, which then received criticism from male classmates and harassment from online trolls. Showing solidarity and defiance toward haters, a number of Icelandic women started freeing their nipples. The campaign has set out to challenge laws and stigmas against topless women when men do not face the same barriers. A global show of support was garnered with women going shirtless in a number of countries, posting pictures on social media of freed nipples along the way.

On exploring the campaign, I found that there is yet to be action with the same momentum which demands that men cover their nipples as an alternative way of equalising torso dressing. I imagine that such a campaign could be equally effective, but requires men to play their part in covering up to gain traction. A mildly hot (even chilly) summer day in the UK demonstrates that we are a long way from covered up male chests being the accepted norm in hot weather.

Guerrilla feminism can certainly drive huge surges of impact for the feminist cause by those who are willing and able to engineer it. However, sometimes it can also cause severe offence and land a very different message, such as Pussy Riot who are well known for deeply offending the Church and many of

Christianity's devoutest followers. Guerrilla campaigns are akin to the effectiveness of the PR stunt; they can work really well or they can go badly wrong. For example, the Free the Nipple campaign has often been criticised for making it easy to objectify women — "You peel off your shirts and make it easier for us to ogle you." Other lesser known campaigns haven't quite had the viral impact that they had wanted such as:

- Protesting the tampon tax in the UK by free-bleeding outside The Houses of Parliament.
- Adding glitter to armpit hair and then posting the photos on social media.
- Posting photos of "peed in my pants" as some activists took to arguing that women should be able to urinate as publicly as men.

There are many other guerrilla campaigns and stunts which did not capture enough people's imaginations. Others have made a real difference, like the #MeToo[38] campaign which has had meaningful local, global and national traction.

For those who don't know, the #MeToo campaign, started as a guerrilla movement against sexual harassment and sexual assault. #MeToo spread virally in October 2017 as a hashtag used on social media in an attempt to demonstrate the widespread prevalence of sexual assault and harassment, especially in the workplace. It followed soon after the sexual misconduct allegations against American film producer, Harvey Weinstein.

Guerrilla activism is needed because it often takes collective fervoured action to ensure that a lasting point is made and then acted upon. In October 2017 I was the winner of a coveted award by a national trade body association. For clarity, not linked in any way to my current employer, but to some pro-bono work I was doing. After I had collected my trophy, the winners of all of the awards that night (there were five people including me who were all women plus one man) were asked to go back on stage for a group photo with a senior leader in the association. Let's call him, Lee.

Rather than offering words of encouragement, support or even praise (we had won some very prestigious awards after all), Lee said, "I get to be the only man (he ignored the male winner!) on stage with you. I feel like Harvey Weinstein with his girls." He quickly followed up with, "Oooops, perhaps shouldn't have said that" when my face instinctively threw him a very annoyed look. Needless to say that I am not smiling in that photo which ended up in various newspapers and magazines. Lee's conduct was totally derogatory and it bemuses me to this day how he has managed to get away with such glib and sexist language in his leadership position. But then, many men have, which is exactly what the #MeToo campaign is addressing.

Not everyone is a natural guerrilla, and not everyone needs to be. But for those who need or want to bare their guerrilla teeth, I and many other feminists worldwide, welcome it and support it.

For Each Other: Toolkit Action 18

Everyday activism

Women need government support too. And we need more women in government itself. It's important to be vocal about the changes that we want to see and lobby the government to ensure that it takes real action in achieving women's economic, social and political empowerment. We must work hard, have the right attitude and claim our space.

For example, if you believe that period poverty is an issue, encourage your workplace or local shopping centres to provide sanitary protection in their washrooms for free. Or if you see adverts for Christmas gifts where girls are exclusively being steered towards toy vacuums and boys are exclusively being steered towards toy cars then call it out. If you see a safety sign amongst the roadworks saying, Men At Work, then raise it with the local Council.

I worked for a company which held an annual awards evening for its colleagues. Anyone who won an award was invited up on stage to collect a trophy from the Chief Executive. When a man won an award he would also be greeted with a handshake and a bottle of fizz and when a woman won an award she got a hug and kiss on the cheek as well as a bunch of flowers. I spoke to the Chief about this one day, respectfully pointing out that I thought it was sexist. Even though no harm was meant, men and women were being treated differently. I asked the Chief if he would consider kissing everyone who collected an award or shake hands with everyone instead. My everyday activism of highlighting the issue had a small effect: it made him think. The answer to my question, however, was an emphatic "No". But I did make the said Chief think. Hopefully that will instigate further thought and possible change in the future.

For Each Other: Toolkit Action 19

Think and take action to unite

Feminist activists in both Iceland and Kuwait have demonstrated that women need a cause to unite around that captures universal attention. Uniting behind a single cause ensures that gender equality is improved through the very act of unification. What that cause is, matters less than the traction gained as an output of widespread unity.

Think. What could be the cause or trigger that women in your community or country can unite around? Identify what this might be and prepare to take advantage of the moment when it arises. Preparation needs to be in place to take action in a timely and effective way.

Women empowering women is a change that is already taking place with feminist fervour across the world. It is also a change which can accelerate faster than we ever thought possible if every member of womankind joins in with the numerous calls for unification.

There are many ways in which you can be an active feminist and support the end of gender inequality. Whether it is leading or following, action in some degree is necessary from all of womankind. Feminism has many guises. As long as we recognise this and support each other we have hope for an ever happier future.

Don the abaya. Ditch the abaya. Rock a bikini. Rip up a bikini. Feminism can take us in many different directions but each direction leads to the goal of gender equality. The best thing you can do is to be your own kind of feminist and speak up about why and how.

Don't just tolerate differences; value them. Feminists lead change best when they are themselves. For example, you will never ever catch me rubbing glitter in to my armpits, but I respect and welcome other women's right to do so in their quest to advocate for a gender equal world.

Hear from Nasira Habib

Nasira is the Founder and Executive Director of Khoj – Society for People's Education and Khoj – Research and Publication Centre which are based in the world's third most populous country of Pakistan. She has many life achievements which have been centred on the empowerment of women and girls, particularly in supporting people to work their way out of poverty.

Nasira said of her educational work, *"I am pleased to share that I was able to develop an alternative approach and methodology which helped girls and women analyse their situation, identify the root causes of their problems and take action. Hundreds of women went through the learning process and found an alternative self-image which was positive and self-assuring. I can never forget one of my student's words when she said, 'Before you came, I had never thought I was also a human being the same way as men are. Only now, I realise I am also a human being. I used to cook fresh meat for my husband and only make cheap chutney for myself because I always thought men needed more energy.' In the process of finding a method of teaching literacy in the shortest period of time, I was able to develop a fast track method of teaching Urdu and other provincial languages. This was a big achievement and I am convinced if this method is employed, the huge problem of illiteracy in Pakistan can be tackled in two to three years."*

At the request of a Pakistani women's program, she went on to develop a whole suite of learning materials for children based on the principles of relevance, gender equity and integration. Later, she went on to develop learners' content and teachers' guides for non-formal education. Through this work, Nasira was able to revolutionise the lives of girls and women in one of the worst crime hit areas in Pakistan. When she started work in the villages of Sheikhupura in Punjab in 1999, she could only find one high school educated woman. There were no roads, no functional schools and no dispensaries. Nasira recalls that the men in the villages had no qualms in saying that women were born to serve the men. "A woman is like a shoe. One can change it when one desires, " was the common thinking. Girls' education was neither important nor desirable; the skill of reading and writing could deem them immoral, according to local beliefs. It was a long journey but Nasira can now say with a huge degree of satisfaction that as a result of her efforts and those of her team, that hundreds of girls and women were able to complete their high school education. Many of them earned bachelors and masters degrees as well. More importantly, more than twenty women who were graduates of the education programme are now teaching at various educational facilities and empowering even more girls themselves.

Linked to the above is another empowerment achievement. Crime was a way of life in the villages. Young and old were involved in killing, dacoity, theft, endless litigation and all kinds of social evils. The boys who studied at Khoj School were able to have a firm educational foundation which motivated a number of them to go for higher education studies and there are others who have since been successfully working for businesses either in Pakistani cities or in the Middle East. That means the interventions of the school contributed considerably in the decline of the crime rate in the area.

When the Khoj team started working in the villages of Sheikhupura under Nasira's leadership, they were seen as a bunch of unqualified women who wanted to teach women and girls. The teachers were perceived as insignificant and powerless. However, over the years, they were able to make significant cultural inroads to establish their credibility and presence to further the cause of women's development.

"I must share with you my first public protest," said Nasira. "It was 1975, the UN women's year. I was fifteen years old and this was my first year at college. Zulfiqar Ali Bhutto was the Prime Minister of Pakistan. His government wanted all educational institutions to celebrate a women's day. There was such excitement among the girls and teachers and the preparations were at their climax. And then there was anti-climax! We were told that the event was cancelled because the governor of Punjab had received sixty telegrams from the clergy saying that on women's day some immoral activities were going to take place. We protested, protested and protested. Finally, we won and the event did take place but it became more of an anti-clergy affair. Girls would come on stage and recite poetry against them. That first collective protest which ended in victory was a very positive, empowering experience.

Women's empowerment requires self-belief, a positive self-image, economic independence and the ability to take decisions. However, this empowerment cannot take place in a vacuum. There must be women's solidarity groups and supporting state institutions which provide support and an enabling environment, in the absence of which it is difficult to achieve any semblance of empowerment.

As the German philosopher Hegel explained: a slave hates the master because the slave lost his freedom because of the master but despite the hatred, his ideal is the master and he aspires to be like him. Likewise, in patriarchal societies, those women who fight for their rights and champion the cause of women as leaders have men as their role models because they have absorbed the dynamics of power mongering practised by men, right from their childhoods. Therefore, they jealously guard their power positions to remain at the helm of affairs and close doors to other women. Every woman must take a responsibility to create a culture of trust and power sharing. Solidarity and unity among women can make them a formidable power to be reckoned with. The anti-women laws during the draconian rule of Zia ul Haq gave birth to a women's movement which protested against the injustice. Women from elitist families in the national and provincial capital cities ran a campaign against the discriminatory laws. With the end of the dictatorship, the movement lost its momentum. There were a lot of ownership issues but the greatest problem was the confinement of the movement to the upper middle class. There was no effort made to mobilise women and men across classes."

Nasira's personal advice to women is to unite and have confidence. It is especially key to support each other in all circumstances. To help each other to overcome encumbrances faced in everyday life. To rise above petty jealousies and have a focus on issues rather than people. Women must remember that *"nothing in us is a disadvantage"*. Remember that your contribution to families, countries and the world is immense. She urges us all to:

"Be a beneficiary of your own hard work. Treat yourself well, and the world will treat you well."[39]

Hear From Farah Alali

Farah Alali lives in Kuwait and has a portfolio career. She is a Computer Engineer and a Television Presenter. She has hosted a diverse range of shows on computing, women's issues, children's shows and chat shows. Currently, alongside her engineering work, she is also learning about meteorology and presents the weather on Kuwaiti television. She is the first female to ever present the weather for her television channel. This is what Farah has to say about becoming a presenter:

"My passion is finding out what people do and also why they do it. People's stories are so varied and different. I love learning from them and hope that my viewers will also learn about other viewpoints; maybe even judge other people less as a consequence.

In Kuwaiti society people think that presenting is not the ideal job for a woman. Parents often worry about the potential for women being on the receiving end of sexual harassment in this job, and therefore don't encourage their daughters to be presenters. Because of this, we have a lot of non-Kuwaitis doing the job. Very few local girls do it but I hope that things are changing. People think that being a television presenter involves flirting and attracting unnecessary attention so this has become a taboo job for Kuwaitis.

In my time at the news channel men have always been respectful. No-one has ever crossed the line. I make the effort to tell people that if they are worried about sexual harassment then they need to address that issue with the men who they worry may cause the perpetration. It's not right to penalise the women. My crew is great and if any misdemeanours ever did occur I would feel confident escalating the issues to my manager. I know that I would get taken seriously and that the issues would be dealt with. The role has been taboo because of fear and not because of actual harassment.

I think it's a shame that independent women are feared by both sexes; many men are afraid of them and many women think that they are too daring. My parents were very supportive of my job. I had to explain to them why I wanted to be on television and my mum was instantly supportive. However, she did say that I had to get permission from my dad. He had to allow it, for me to get the family's support. Even now a lot of my friends say, "How was your dad ok with your decision?" Culturally women still need to get approval from the head man in her family for big decisions like jobs and travelling although there is no legislation in place any more to endorse this.

One of the reasons I love my work as a presenter is because it is so visible. It means I get lots of recognition for what I do. People will often come up to me and say, "Hey, I saw you on TV. I love the show." I love my engineering work too but it doesn't have the same levels of public recognition which I feel women should get more of. It's very nice to be recognised and appreciated for your work and contribution to society.

I also support my friends and co-workers through volunteering my time. In Kuwait we are privileged as there is no poverty. However, there is loneliness. I'm doing volunteering for the psychiatry centre. I work with female patients; a lot of them are old women and feel abandoned with no-one to visit. On a weekly basis me and my friends go there to cheer them up. We listen to music, do their make-up and draw and paint with them. They look forward to our visits.

There was a campaign to recruit for the centre called, "Mind Me" run by a female doctor who felt that patients needed support as they didn't get any willing visitors. One patient didn't even have her kids visit her as her ex-husband stopped them from seeing her. The female doctor wanted them to socialise to support their mental health. I joined in because I felt like it was my time to give back to the community given my position in society and what I have been kindly given myself by others. I wanted to do something good. Recently the doctor said that there is a huge improvement in how the patients are feeling because they are socialising with people. They are healthier and happier.

For me, women's empowerment is all about supporting one another as females. We should be strong and independent. We need people to encourage us and respect decisions that we make for ourselves.

The secret to living, I believe, is giving."

The Clothing Conundrum

Part 11

Burkas, Burkinis and Bikinis

It will be no surprise to anyone that both the burka and the bikini are clothing items of huge contention across the world. The burka, largely seen as a cloak of female oppression by a number of European countries as demonstrated through law, and the bikini, viewed as an item which demeans women by many Arabic and Asian countries also demonstrated through the law. How a woman chooses to clothe or not clothe her body is legislated in a way that men's bodies are not.

In countries such as Saudi Arabia, Kuwait, the UAE, Pakistan and Iran the burka, a head covering which also covers the shoulders is commonplace. Although it is not an Islamic requirement, the burka has mainly been worn in very conservative Muslim cultures. Young girls are not required to cover themselves with a burka, but at puberty they may begin to wear it. Whilst women do not often wear the burka while they are at home with their families, they are, in a number of countries, required to wear it (either legally or culturally depending on where in the world they are) when they are in public or in the presence of men who are not family members. Though the burka can appear confining, many devout Muslim women freely choose to wear it. Often women say that the coverage of the burka gives them a privacy that actually makes them feel freer to move about in society. Also, many Muslim women who live in very conservative societies are forced to patriarchally wear the burka whether they want to or not, and many have been punished harshly for refusing to cover themselves as their local laws demand.

In countries such as Pakistan, where the burka is not a legal requirement, it is also worn by Christian and Sikh women as it is more about a cultural norm of dressing modestly. Modest dressing is in fact a part of the Christian faith and the Sikh faith. A common misconception is that Muslim women are the only ones who cover their hair. It may be true that Islam is the only religion in which most women seem to follow its directives to cover the hair, but it is not the only gender or religion to have such directives. In Saudi Arabia, men also wear a head covering in public, both for the purposes of modesty and to keep cool.

On a recent trip to Alicante in Spain, I was treated to the visual feast of the city's weekend long Fiesta. There were parades and marches every night where women and girls were dressed in traditional clothing, including what could be described as a white lace hijab or headscarf. This included toddlers and more senior members of the community and the headscarves were also widely available in most local clothing stores as an everyday item available for purchase. I had not expected to see this, mainly because head coverings for non-muslim women are not demonised in the European media the way that Muslim head coverings are.

Debates over whether to ban the burka often assume that women are forced by men to wear it. In many Muslim countries, women lack equality and basic rights that other women take for granted; therefore, the burka may seem to be one more example of patriarchal control. I recently visited Saudi Arabia on an Umrah (pilgrimage) visa and although I was looking forward to the trip I was also terrified about getting in to trouble with the Saudi authorities by accidentally breaking the law. I had heard all sorts of horror stories about policing, such as visitors being imprisoned for having cough medicine in their luggage (as it contains alcoholic ingredients); women being sent to jail for taking a taxi without a male chaperone, and being beaten with a police baton for a hair slipping out from under the hijab. I am ashamed to say that I was truly terrified. Terrified, because of what I had read in the British media. Ashamed, because what I experienced was very different to what I was expecting.

The hijab, as a head covering is legally mandatory in Saudi Arabia, but the burka which is a more intense covering, is not. I was apprehensive about wearing a head scarf for two weeks straight and worried about what I would look like (even though everyone else would look just the same). I ordered numerous coverings which I personally deemed as modestly fashionable only to later decide to embrace the experience fully and go for a suitcase of full-on burkas and abayas instead. I was dressed the part for my trip from checking in for my flight at Manchester airport to staying in Saudi for two weeks and then landing back at Manchester airport.

For weeks I had been worried about what I would experience in Saudi Arabia, but the bitterest experience was actually at Manchester airport. I hadn't expected that wearing a headscarf would reduce my perceived intelligence to the outside world. The ladies on security spoke to me fifty decibels louder than to anyone else and signed through hand movements and strange body shaking to tell me to take my jewellery off before I passed through the scanners. At the premium make-up counters in the duty free zones, where I normally get approached within seconds and get pitched the latest new blusher or lipstick I was avoided, even when there were no other customers. Getting served became a challenge I had never experienced before. All of a sudden, my fellow British females assumed that I had diminished intelligence and an empty purse. It was a mortifying experience and yet I was grateful to get a snapshot in to how women who wear the burka are often made to feel.

Stupidity isn't the only thing which people can hallucinate in a burka wearing woman; they can be mocked and social media bullied as well. On my last visit to Abu Dhabi in the United Arab Emirates, I was swimming in the hotel pool in my burkini (a swimming costume which has full length sleeves and leggings attached). This shouldn't have come as a surprise to any guests in the hotel as we were in Arabia after all. However, I noticed that a group of bikini clad guests who were relaxing on the sun loungers were actually having a fierce cackle and filming me. I was the only burkini wearing woman at the pool that day. I wouldn't have minded them observing my outfit as a novelty to visitors not used to seeing modest swimming gear; but to laugh, point and film me was an unsettling and upsetting experience. I'm pretty sure that the video the female onlookers took of me that day probably ended up on a social media site so that their friends at home could have a laugh too. I got the same treatment at Hoar Cross Hall, a luxurious spa in Staffordshire where I decided to relax in a tankini and leggings instead of a bikini. I have to say that it ruined the relaxing as being laughed at is not much fun at all.

Back to my Saudi trip. I found the hijab strange and uncomfortable for a couple of days due to the swathes of material and it making me feel extra warm, but then after that it became an easy part of my daily dressing routine. I was able to get ready in a flash as donning a hijab is tens of minutes quicker than straightening my hair and I enjoyed the shared identity with the other women on the same trip as me.

There is no doubt that the country is hugely sexist. Men are served first in shops and restaurants. Men have better rest areas and facilities. Men can drive without going to prison for it. But I found my alternative way of dressing liberating as after a week my brain had stopped placing an enormous amount of importance on how I looked and I was able to focus on my Umrah and enjoying the delights of Makkah and Medinah instead.

I also got laughed at in Saudi though, this time by the concierge. When I enquired about whether I could get a taxi as a female travelling without a male because I had heard that the penalty for doing so was prison or being beheaded, I was faced with a loud roar of laughter. It turns out that what I had heard was an urban myth and I was able to take a taxi at 3am in the morning with a male taxi driver feeling perfectly safe for the most part. Sadly though, the burka did not protect me from unwanted male attention on a number of occasions. The first time was when a man, dressed in full traditional Arab dress, thrust a camera in my face in a lift and tried to take a photo of me.

The second time, when a man, again in full Arab dress, pulled his car up next to me as I was walking along the street and tried to beckon me in to his car. Despite being a kingdom which decrees modesty I was treated poorly by the men in the country.

On the other end of the clothing contention scale is the bikini. Many women feel that showing more skin makes them feel empowered. This is because they are expressing their sexual agency in a society that can attempt to repress women's sexuality. Showing skin can challenge patriarchal norms, for example, the fact that women in many countries can now wear more revealing clothing shows that the heavy emphasis on policing women's sexuality is gradually being removed. However, women who do dare to bare all in a bikini can often be body-shamed and stigmatised for not having a slim and toned figure. A scan of magazine covers on the shelves of two New York supermarkets, two Birmingham supermarkets and two Sydney supermarkets revealed that having an idealised "bikini body" is still very much a part of our everyday vernacular. Here's a flavour of some topical tips to carry out before donning a bikini which I found during the summer of 2018:

• "In addition to eating fish the week leading up to a bikini-worthy event for its protein and anti-inflammatory Omega-3 fat qualities, I always eat asparagus. It is a natural diuretic that helps lean you out. Avoid grains and dairy at all costs—both will majorly bloat you." **Shannon, United States**

• "Make a vision board. Funny as that sounds, your thoughts have just as much power as your actions.

Keeping images of clothes, people, body types, and things that you admire will help you gravitate to acquiring those attributes if you reinforce them constantly. It can really help you accomplish your goals—fitness and otherwise!" **Priya, Designer**

- "I love adding silicone bra inserts to my suit! It makes me look proportioned and gives me great cleavage. I also like to apply a nice bronzer or self-tanner to firm up the skin and get a touch of summer glow, and I love to pair my swimsuit with a great wedge sandal. Wedge sandals give your legs an amazing look (lean and slim) and also help your posture. Even though it's hard to walk in the sand with wedges ... it's a great look for the boardwalk or lounging around in your beach bungalow or cabana." **Christina, Model**

The majority of headlines, articles, blogs and television programmes I examined (over a thousand) were all focussed on how women could achieve a bikini body through either losing weight, toning up, bronzing up or cleverly hiding belly and leg fat. I did however come across ten articles which talked about the bikini body being anybody's body. Kayla Itsines, one of the world's most famous Personal Trainers, says that everybody has a bikini body, "And there isn't one type". If you can physically put a bikini on then essentially that's a bikini body. To many women, it means feeling confident when they're wearing their least.

- **Kat, a Beauty Blogger**, says of bikinis, "When I put on a bikini it represents my taking the power back to love my body after years of being body shamed and bullied. It's empowering as a plus-size woman to proudly wear garments deemed unsuitable just because I weigh more. This bikini is my statement to the world that I will not be ashamed of my body, that I will take up space and wear whatever I please. Life is too short to spend it hating your body and summers are too hot to hide under layers so I hope this helps inspire women to go out and rock that bikini they have been dreaming of whatever size they may wear! Female nudity in both fashion and society at large continues to create tension among feminists; debating between notions of objectification and empowerment." Kat's work became popular because she is relatable to so many women.

- **Lindsay, a Writer**, says, "This year, instead of thinking the worst about yourself and your body, let your bikini be a symbol of strength, acceptance and beauty, celebrating the unique shape, curves and imperfections that make you shine."

- **Michelle, a Body Confidence Coach** says, "I have had 15 surgeries, a brain tumour, a brain cyst, a punctured intestine, an obstructed bowel, and a condition called hydrocephalus, and for many years, I always hid my scars. When I was 21 though, I decided to become a life coach and specialise in body confidence. In doing so, I realised this was the last battle I had to face in terms of my confidence. I wore a bikini for the first time and launched my campaign "Scarred Not Scared" on Instagram to talk about surgery scars and unveil the silence that often surrounds chronic illness." Michelle's work became popular because she is relatable to a specific group of women.

What is often forgotten in discussions on bikinis is that it has a clear technical function as well as a social and body image function. That is, allowing a woman to tan her entire body whilst covering her most intimate areas. The bikini allows a greater tan coverage than a tankini or one-piece swimsuit. Many women also find that they are easier to wear and more practical for swimming than a one-piece. Men also face some pressure to get a beach ready body but the debate is never as prolific as for women, where all segments of society and the commercial world pitch in with their views on what a "bikini body" really is.

The decision about what and how a woman chooses to dress should be hers and hers alone. It's when that choice is taken away or stereotyped that the conversation becomes one of oppression and not empowerment. Having travelled across many countries, I can confidently say that the world holds one thing in common, and that is the prolific discussion on women's bodies. Attitudes to covering up or bare-ing all differ across countries, but the fact remains that women's bodies and to what extent they are covered is a common conversational topic everywhere. This includes obsessions on how we perceive other cultures, nationalities and religions perceiving women's bodies, which often leads to misrepresentation in itself. It is also fair to say that women's bodies are discussed so much more than the male form. I'm sure that hearing these discussions is something that we can all relate to.

In 2016 I was supported by the UK government's Department of International Trade for an export visit to Kuwait. I was due to meet a number of Middle Eastern companies such as Al Yasra and Al Shaya, as well as Western based companies operating out of Kuwait under franchise, including brands such as Harvey Nichols and Debenhams.

The British Embassy in Kuwait had set up a number of meetings with key businesses I wanted to target and so I took the task of preparing my brand collateral for these meetings very seriously. Months of effort went in to designing, producing and then printing brand books and new collection materials especially for the Kuwaiti market. All of my market research pointed to a sense of female modesty and so I ensured that whilst the images in my brand materials showed an amount of leg skin, ankles and bare arms, they were modest enough for the meetings. In any case, they were much more modest than my UK brand materials.

Two weeks before I was due to depart I had a meeting scheduled with a Department of International Trade representative who was a culture expert for the Middle East. It is fair to say that the meeting did not go how I thought it would. I had expected to get some good feedback on being proactive in translating my materials to Arabic and on making the imagery country appropriate.

I was sent away from The Chamber of Commerce to remove all visible aspects of female flesh except the tops of the feet which the shoes did not cover and to tone down the legs shown in images. I was instructed that I would need to have a scarf to wear in public even if I was wearing a trouser suit which covered my legs and arms and warned to avoid tights and stick to thick leggings as long as my dress came below my knees. The next weeks were a whirlwind of stress for me and my Graphic Designer as we reworked all the materials whilst I shopped for the prescribed wardrobe items for myself. But when I actually got to Kuwait I was in for another shock. My preparations based on my market research, and the preparations done for me by the government's international culture experts were ...... terribly amiss.

My experience in Kuwait was a tight mesh of two clothing cultures which co-existed in calm acceptance. I saw hundreds of local Kuwaiti women dressed in abayas, many in headscarves and some in full-on niqab face coverings. I also saw the same amount of local Kuwaiti women dressed in revealing lace mini-dresses and spaghetti strap silk tops; in public. The one thing that the women had in common across the two groups, as far as I could see, was wealth. In modern day Kuwait, natural born Kuwaitis who are born in to poverty are few and far between, if not non-existent. Whether she was wearing a flowing black abaya or a thigh skimming lace dress, it was hard to miss the shine of the Cartier bracelets, Chanel handbags and the highest of designer skyscraper heels.

Far from being backwards in fashion as is often perceived by people living outside of Kuwait, the country hosts one of the world's largest shopping centres called The Avenues from where many designer pieces can be picked up before they are released in the fashion capitals of Paris, Milan,

London or New York. It was also exhilarating to experience that there was no overt body shaming or oppressive sneering as the various clothing cultures were happily in co-existence.

The other surprise to me was the functional benefit of an abaya. I had purchased a dressy purple one for my trip with masses of material which covered every inch of my body from neck to wrists and feet. I wasn't expecting to wear it much given that I had arrived in a belting fifty degrees centigrade heat, but, my oh my, was I wrong! The abaya became my most worn item for the two weeks that I was there because of how practical it was to wear in the heat. The flowing materials kept me cool and sun safe as well as being more bearable to wear in the heat. The men had also, quite literally, cottoned on to the robe being practical and weather worthy. Many wore cotton robes covering their entire bodies whilst others wore trouser suits or shorts and t-shirts. Nobody bared their chests, male or female, when on the beach. There was not a single point during the trip where I needed to wear a scarf.

And then there came my experience of the Kuwaiti business meetings. Whether it was a Middle Eastern business, or the likes of Harvey Nichols, no-one batted an eyelid at female flesh in adverts. In fact, my two weeks of reworking my brand materials were unnecessary as in doing so my marketing had in fact become too conservative for Kuwait. I had been told by UK government representatives that women would not be shown in adverts, other than perhaps their face or hands, but this was not the case. The billboards, magazines and television programmes sported a diverse range of women. Whilst there, I was invited to appear on the Kuwaiti news channel to talk about my work on empowering women through sustainable footwear. I was able to wear my shirt and skinny trousers with confidence. To scarf up, or not to scarf, was happily my decision to make even when appearing on prime time television.

The biggest learning I took away from my Kuwaiti preparations and experience was that, despite feeling I had researched well, my expectations of how the female form is viewed did not match the reality. Hours of searching the internet, reading Kuwaiti books and meeting Kuwaiti culture experts based in Britain did not adequately prepare me. There are most definitely gender developments in this desert come metropolis which are not seen by non-Kuwaiti eyes but are a welcome surprise when visiting.

I also discovered that the country is an escape haven from the neighbouring country of Saudi Arabia. Saudis often travel to Kuwait for fashion respite and to shed a few layers for a few hours. In modern day Kuwait, modesty it seems is quite truly an empowering choice. When I retuned to the UK I debriefed the culture advisers on the reality I had experienced. They were surprised at what I had found and yet continue to coach business people on a generic and outdated view of Kuwaiti culture. Entrenched perception, albeit well meaning, takes a long time to change, but it's important to foster the courage to speak out.

My visit to Iceland was also full of surprises. It is perfectly legal for men and women to be nude in

Iceland, as long as no offence is caused to anyone. Iceland's free attitude towards nudity largely stems from a mix of the hot spring and pool culture, traditional folklore, a willingness to experiment with art, and a history of feminist protest. Shy travellers face both a blessing and a curse when it comes to nudity and swimming pools in Iceland.

Locals told me that nudity is perceived as the natural state of a human being; it is, therefore not sexualised, but combined with nature, signifying something pure, innocent and timeless. On the one hand, swimsuits are mandatory in all public pools (not including bikini tops), so you don't need to worry about getting flashed while you're trying to relax. On the other, you are obligated to shower and wash your naked body before you enter the pool. Men and women have an equal chance at getting a tan as only pants are required because both men and women can bare their chests in and around a pool.

However, even in Iceland attitudes to women's breasts versus men's chests have caused contention, giving rise to the guerrilla Free the Nipple campaign. In Iceland there are two things which people are legally not permitted to undress for. The first reason is money. The second is entertainment.

Since 2010, it has been the policy of the government that no person's body is a commodity and, therefore, those who strip for a living, male or female, must leave a fair amount to the imagination of their patrons. This legal move was part of a wider crackdown on prostitution and the sex trade, where those who purchased the services of an escort or were pimping would face charges; but not the escorts themselves. This, in turn, was part of a wider push to modernise Iceland's gender dialogue and face the gendered issues of an increasingly globalised world. Though the legislation has faced criticism from some for being sex-negative, it has also been praised for helping limit the exploitation of women being brought to Iceland specifically to be a part of the sex trade.

One lady called Hilduura, a fashion designer who I met in Iceland, said that, "Regulating how a woman undresses, is little better than telling a woman how to dress. I for one will not be restrained from using my body as a commodity if I so wish. How I use my body; how I dress it and how I undress it should be up to me."

My experience of Iceland was one of calm, peace and respect for women by women and by men. It is a country which is at ease with itself, and the gender empowerment which it holds. The rest of the world, however, is awash with examples of over legislating women's clothing. Consider this[40]:

- **France** was the first European country to ban the burka in public. It started in 2004, with a clampdown on students in state-run schools displaying any form of religious symbol. But in April 2011, the government went further by bringing in a total public ban on full-face veils.

- **Italy** does not have a national ban on the full-face veil, but in 2010, the town of Novara imposed restrictions; though there is currently no established fines system. In some parts of Italy, local authorities have banned burkinis.

- **Turkey**, until 2013, had legislation rules banning women from wearing headscarves in the country's state institutions. Women can now wear the veil everywhere except in the judiciary, military and police.

- **Switzerland** enforced a ban on the full-face veil in July 2016. It means women wearing a burka or niqab could face fines of almost ten thousand euros.

- **Italy** is home to Rome and The Vatican City. The holy Catholic city, and particularly St Peters Basilica, has a strict dress code. Here, shorts or bare shoulders are not allowed for men or women, and women strictly cannot wear miniskirts. It is not negotiable, so if tourists or citizens show up with bare shoulders they will be turned away.

- **Thailand** has made underboob selfies illegal and can get social media addicts in to a whole lot of trouble if they break the ban by posting images of the underside of a breast.

- **Afghanistan** in recent decades has had more periods of time where the burka had to legally be worn by women in public than not. Under Taliban rule, burka wearing was mandatory.

You don't have to look far to find legislation on what to wear or not to wear in any country, more so for women than for men. But as well as legislation, there are also rules to contend with: societal rules, cultural rules, religious rules, fashion rules and underlying all this the varying perceptions of these rules.

For the next clothing debate, please, for the sanity of woman kind … let's make it about a mankini.

For Each Other: Toolkit Action 20

Foster the courage to speak out

Having the courage to speak out and share your thoughts is an important part of being included. It quite literally doesn't pay to stay quiet when you have an idea. All women should have the self belief to put themselves and their thoughts forward in order to inspire others. As women, the first thing that we can do is to speak out ourselves, and the next thing that we can do is give other women the self belief to speak up too. Either through direct encouragement or by being a good role model.

The other important aspect of speaking out is to acknowledge good ideas made by other women. Too often in meetings I have witnessed a woman share an idea which nobody appears to hear with any enthusiasm. Minutes later a man can echo the same point without acknowledging that it is an echo and gain all of the credit and exclamations of praise. When you witness this happen, speak up for your fellow woman.

"It's great that <he> echoed <her> idea and that there is so much enthusiasm around the table. Well done <her name>. A point well made and well received."

You don't have to be a loud mouth. And you don't have to give credit to anyone for what you believe to be a poor idea or approach. But you do have to cut through when it matters.

Speak out in solidarity when it is needed and help other women to stand tall.

For Each Other: Toolkit Action 21

Champion relatable and unrelatable women

Many would-be female entrepreneurs say that seeing and hearing about a relatable role model would encourage them to start their own businesses. Talk about your story when you do something amazing (no cringing we all do amazing things) and champion other women who have great stories to tell too. Helping women to develop a greater sense of self belief is key to ensuring the next generation of female business and political leaders rise up.

There are also women who we may feel are seemingly unrelatable whose stories can inspire more women. Tell these stories too. Our gender unites us and by hearing stories from cultures and geographies totally different to ours we can often learn more than we ever thought possible. For example, an immigrant living in Kuwait may seem unrelatable to women living outside of the Middle East who have not heard of the country, but will likely not seem unrelatable to women who are Arabic or have an Arabic heritage. It can be easy to misunderstand what people are and aren't able to relate to.

For example, recently I went to a British bank to exchange my Kuwaiti Dinars for British Pounds. It was the same bank I had purchased the dinars from. The cashier (and her supervisor) both said that there was no way that they could have issued the dinars in the first place as they hadn't even heard of the country. Of course, producing my initial exchange receipt sorted the confusion which came from presenting a currency which the bank's team were not used to. Some people are great at being able to imagine themselves in different situations, but many aren't. Therefore, it's worth remembering that relatable women and relatable environments will have a more profound impact when delivering an empowerment message.

If you are a leader, then another empowering thing you can do is to look out for the women who need training or coaching on how to stand out and create their own personal brand. A few words of private coaching can go a long way in shaping someone's confidence and presence.

Unequal Food Distribution

Part 12

Food For Female Thought

The day I met Helen Pankhurst she asked a thought provoking question:

"If there was one thing you could do right now to end gender inequality what would it be?"[41]

Helen said that whilst she was completing interviews for her book, Deeds Not Words, she asked that question of a number of women. Some of the ideas she heard from interviewees were:

- *"Charge women less tuition fees at university than men. We get paid less so we should pay less up front. The difference should be reflective of the gender pay gap."*

- *"Women should pay less for a TV license than men. After all, we are not even adequately represented on the BBC and by their own admission the corporation has paid women consistently less than men."*

- *"Make it mandatory to have pockets in women's clothes as often as men's clothes. Imagine the everyday practical freedom that this wardrobe change would bring."*

The interviewees were answering the question relating to the United Kingdom in particular. My own thoughts were related to what I believe is the crux of the problem in the majority of countries, if not all countries at some level, particularly where poverty is concerned. For me, based on what I have seen, read and heard from across the world, inequality manifests itself through the basics of food and water before anything else. Hunger is a major worldwide problem. It affects boys, girls, men and women. Sadly, female hunger is more prominent especially in poverty stricken areas.

If there was one thing I could do to end gender inequality right now it would be to enable fair access to food for females and males. The simple fact is this, that discrimination causes poverty and poverty causes hunger. The gender pay gap exists even in the most equal of countries, such as Iceland, and it is always women who are the gender at the lower end of the pay scale.

Here are the facts on female hunger as cited by the World Hunger Education Service in their Hunger Notes document freely available during 2019:[42]

- Women and girls represent sixty per cent of all undernourished people in the world.

- The United Nations estimates that seventy per cent of the 1.3 billion people in poverty worldwide are women.

- At least 120 million women in developing countries are underweight.

- In some geographies, more women are underweight than not; for example, sixty per cent of women are estimated to be underweight in South Asia.

- Babies born to a malnourished mother are much more likely to have low birth weights. This is one of the strongest predictors of whether a child will die before their fifth birthday.

- In poverty stricken areas, divorce rates have been shown to rise during food shortages. This leaves women and children who have relied on male breadwinners to fend for themselves. In cultures where divorced women are shunned in society, this is particularly bad.

- Food shortages are shown to lead to daughters being married off sooner so there are fewer mouths to feed. Females who are married before reaching adulthood are more likely to end their education early, to become pregnant while malnourished, to die during childbirth, and to give birth to babies with poor health.

- Differences in control of economic resources between men and women, such as landholding and access to credit, hinder the ability of women to cope with rising food prices.

The hunger issue is devastating in countries where there is extreme poverty, but we would be wrong to think that it does not affect gender equality in the United Kingdom and in other wealthy nations.

Economic inequalities are prevalent in the UK, take the gender pay gap for instance. In April 2018 the Financial Times reported that more than three out of four companies in Britain pay their male staff more than their female staff, and in nine out of seventeen sectors in the economy, men earn ten per cent or more on average than women.[43]

Less pay naturally means less money which means that women are often forced to choose between food and other feminine specific essentials such as sanitary protection. Period poverty has been widely reported in Europe over the last two years, whereas in prior years it was something which was perceived as happening in countries with the lowest wealth levels. Within the last decade, I am proud to have worked at a leading British health and beauty retailer which lead the way in lobbying government for the removal of Value Added Tax from sanitary products. As of 2018, when purchasing sanitary towels or tampons in the UK women pay five per cent tax as they are deemed non essential items. From 2017, the majority of supermarkets and health product retailers scrapped the five per cent tax by funding it themselves and lowering prices of the products to relieve the pains of period poverty. The average cost of a period in the UK in 2019 is five hundred pounds per woman per year. Research by the maker of Always sanitary products, showed a fifth of UK parents struggled to afford sanitary protection for their daughters. In addition to this, more than one hundred and thirty five thousand girls missed out on school in some way each year because of period poverty; this in one of the wealthiest nations in the world. In the world's poorest nations the figures are atrocious when it comes to both food and periods.

In my work within the business world, I have seen first hand the inequalities that girls and women face when it comes to food, and therefore education, finance, politics and independence. The profits from every pair of shoes sold through my company, Shoes by

Shaherazad, supports a woman or girl to gain an education in order to lift herself out of poverty. Currently, the women I have sent funding to are based in Peru, Pakistan, Palestine, Kenya, Jordan, Yemen, Syria, Bangladesh and my home country of the UK. Poverty is everywhere in some form or another and I would love for it to be non-existent across the world.

My reason for sharing my brand ethos is as follows. I feel a strong responsibility to enable as many women and girls as I possibly can to end the gender inequality gap. I feel a need to enable women to make their own life choices which in turn will enable happier and equal societies. My preference is for the money which is given to the women and girls to be used for educational purposes as this is proven to have the most sustainable effect, empowering all areas of their lives. However, oftentimes the money is invested in simple food: porridge, nuts, seeds, soup or even the necessity of clean water. It is important that women and girls are given opportunities like this to make decisions about their own finances themselves.

It is food which more often than not gives parents the enablement in poverty stricken countries to send their daughters to school instead of sending them to collect grains of rice scattered amongst the sand. It is food which gives girls the energy to walk thirty miles to school and thirty miles back again, without which they would not have been physically able to make the journey. It is food which gives poverty stricken parents the incentive to allow girls to invest in their education which in turn allows them to go out and earn a living to feed even more hungry mouths.

Some of the projects supported by my company have used their funds to provide bowls of hot porridge to families on condition that the girls attend school. Others have used it to feed teachers so that they are able to attend and focus on the task at hand, many of whom teach for little or no pay.   One project was forced through circumstance to use the funds for Plumpy Nut, which is a branded peanut based paste used for the treatment of severe acute malnutrition. It supports rapid weight gain derived from broad nutrient intake which can save a starving child from severe illness or even death. Without exception there is one thing that all of the projects have in common, and that is the goal of the enablement of women and girls to provide themselves with an educationally sound and financially stable future. Female poverty, female education, female hunger and female equality are intrinsically linked.

To achieve a gender equal world I believe that we need to invest in feeding women and girls as much as men and boys. Feeding female bodies and feeding female minds must be an immediate priority.

Politically, culturally, socially and economically.

For Each Other: Toolkit Action 22

Feed the world, including all of the women

Female discrimination is a serious issue which even affects the amount of food we eat or how often women and girls feel hunger pains. Think hard about the issue of food as it lies at the heart of solving many empowerment issues. A bowl of porridge a day can mean the difference between no education and a full time school education. We all need a fair amount of food and nutrition to fuel our day.

Hear from Laurine

Shoes by Shaherazad supports two projects in Kenya. One of them is named the, Girls Empowerment Centre in Kisumu. The Programme Co-ordinator, feminist Godfrey Okumu, shared in his own words the story of one of the girls who attends the centre:

"Laurine is a twenty three year old, Girls Empowerment Centre beneficiary who comes from an informal community in Kisumu County. She got married at the age of sixteen. She recalls the struggle she went through in marriage, and says she can vividly count the number of days she was happy as a woman of the house. These were few and far between.

Laurine's life took a drastic turn in the year 2002 when her father died and her mother had to re-marry. Life with her stepfather was never easy. The stepfather never bothered about her schooling. She had to drop out of school as parental support was never there. When things heated up and she could not stand it anymore, she decided to go and live with her grandmother. Life there had its challenges as well. She later on decided to get married because she thought her life would change for the better.

In her marriage, Laurine had two children. She was happy to have two boys with the man she wanted to spend her entire life with. She never thought their love for each other would fade. As days went by, her husband became abusive, he would beat her and use vulgar insults. He would constantly tell her to go and get educated like other girls. 'My husband would come home in the evening from work empty-handed and whenever I asked him for cash to buy meals he would remind me of how uneducated I was,' said Laurine, recalling her life then. 'My sons and I went several nights without meals, even porridge for my two sons was by chance,' she added.

When it was too much for her to bear, she decided to go back to her parents' home with her children and tried living under the same roof with her stepfather but it was still not easy so she took her children back to their father and returned to her spousal home.

One day, a proactive Field Assistant from the Girls Empowerment Centre went to their home and had a chat with her. The Assistant took her through some of the programmes the centre runs. Laurine got interested in joining and was admitted into the dressmaking and design class. While at the Centre, Laurine's thirst for education was rejuvenated. She interacted more with fellow young women who came over to coach the girls on career choices, job seeking strategies, job interviewing skills, and life planning skills.

'Whenever I reflect on my past and what I have gone through, I get motivated to thrive for a better future, a future where I would not depend on someone for help, a future where I can make my own decisions, a future where I can pay my own bills, a future where I will not depend on a man to be happy,' said Laurine in a sombre mood. The only way for me to realise this dream for the future is through education and that is why I also decided to go back to school," she added.

Laurine registered as a private candidate for the Kenya Certificate of Primary Education at Nyamasaria Adult Learning Centre in Kisumu. Whenever she was not attending her dressmaking and design classes at the Centre, she would be at Nyamasaria for coaching or revising for her exams. She took her classes seriously and despite staying out of school previously for over seven years, she grasped the subjects pretty quickly. She sat her national examinations in 2017 and scored 286 marks out of the possible 500 marks (the pass mark is 250). Laurine hopes to join Secondary School next year and her dream is to become a celebrated fashion designer in the future.

She has also completed her dressmaking and design course and graduated in December. Her apt skills in sewing have earned her customers who mostly send orders for shopping bags. With the ban of plastic bags in Kenya, Laurine has made good fortune from making and selling shopping bags and uses parts of the income to sustain her stay at the Centre and saves part for her secondary education." [44]

Hear from Sheyla

Another project which Shoes by Shaherazad works with is based in Lima in Peru. The project is called La Casa de Panchita. Half a million women and girls work as servants in Peru. Most come to Lima from rural poverty or shanty towns. Girls as young as nine serve as live-in servants to families not their own to earn a meal. They care for young children, foregoing their own education. La Casa de Panchita allows girls the chance to reclaim some of their childhood through educational and recreational support. It also enables women to improve job skills, as they learn to negotiate better employment conditions through basic educational skills. Theresa Zimmer works at the project and shared this story about one of the girls under the care of the empowerment project.

"Imagine an eight year old girl. She is thin, with long dark hair, beautifully shy eyes and is barely as tall as my hips. When she looks at me it seems like she is asking for something without saying a word. Today I had the pleasure of meeting her. Her name is Sheyla.

Sheyla is used to following the instructions of her employing family. She doesn't have any idea of what it means to be responsible, but she is. She doesn't think about the other things she could be doing, playing and living the life of a normal girl, she just does what is needed from her. Her shy, prying eyes seem to ask, 'what do you want me to do? How should I behave?'.

The moment this girl first attracted my attention was at lunch one sunny afternoon. Every Sunday children come from the District of San Juan de Miraflores to enjoy a day of activities and fun in La Casa de Panchita. To go along with the activities, there are also daily programs where the girls learn about domestic work, talk about their rights, the dangers of their work, and useful behaviour in certain situations. There are also some theatrical plays in which they have the opportunity to talk about their experiences and share with each other. In the end there is always a creative activity like making crafts and advent calendars, coupling fun with important life skills and learning. Every Sunday at 1pm there's lunch for everyone.

Sheyla was sitting in front of me at the other end of the table. We had pasta with tomato sauce. There was a huge amount of pasta on every plate. Everybody finished silently, besides Sheyla. She was watching her plate once again with eyes asking, 'what do you want me to do with this?' It was obvious that this was more than too much for her to finish herself, but she tried to continue eating. As she was the last one to finish, everybody was gazing at her and asking her, 'Don't you like it? Are you full? Or do you just need some time to finish?'

Suddenly there were tears in her eyes. So many questions about her simple interest in eating or not eating. She couldn't answer. She never knew what she herself wanted to do. She only did what she was told. So she continued eating while more and more tears silently rolled over her cheeks. Finally someone removed her plate because it was time to go upstairs for our activity to do the handicraft advent calendar. Silently, still a bit scared and troubled she followed the group.

Upstairs at the table, I sat next to her. As she saw all the coloured decorating material like the bright glitter and vibrant paint, her eyes widened. She found a small stencil of a butterfly and asked me if I would help her to paint it on her calendar. "Which colour do you like?", I asked. She raised her eyes and smiled, 'Pink! I like pink!' So together we decorated her calendar with a pink butterfly.

This was the moment when her timidness broke. Just to be able to have fun, to tell me what she liked and to have some control was enough for her. Now she seemed to be just a little girl with long, dark hair, a thin figure, with beautiful, shy but smiling eyes." [45]

All Sheyla needed was a little nudge to empower her with the confidence to think for herself.

Hear from In'am

Shoes by Shaherazad works with an empowerment project which is based in Palestine where hunger, religious apartheid and other inequalities are rife. Tomorrow's Youth Organisation provides female entrepreneurs from marginalised communities with training in business and personal skills required to launch and sustain a commercial enterprise. This in turn empowers women and their families to break the cycle of poverty, further advancing the role of women in their communities. Here, Rawan Musameh who is the organisation's Programme Assistant, tells the story of one of the female entrepreneurs in her own words:

"In'am was born and raised in Jamaa'en, Nablus. She studied mathematics at An-Najah National University and has been working with the Jamaa'en Governmental Municipality for over nine years. In'am needed an additional source of income and decided to transform her long time hobby into a sustainable business. With the money she saved from her job at the municipality, In'am decided to purchase three calves. Initially, she focused her business strictly on the process of fattening and selling her calves. In'am would buy the calves when they were one-week old, feed them for six to eight months, and sell them once they weighed enough. As In'am generated her first profit, she used it to purchase more calves.

In'am's interest in Tomorrow's Youth Organisation's entrepreneur program for women was sparked when representatives from TYO visited the Jamaa'en Women's Association to present the project and recruit entrepreneurs from her village. While In'am had been running an effective, profitable business, there was always a chaotic element. She had never created a business plan and had only operated her business on a day-to-day basis. She needed assistance to identify the source of the chaos and address it.

When the training began, In'am was eager to learn how to develop a business plan. She learned how to develop sound and comprehensive business, marketing, and financial plans. During financial planning training, she began to understand the purpose behind documenting all of the expenses and income of the business. She also learned through psychosocial training that she must document the money spent paying family for their labour as an expense.

Through the Idea Sourcing and Product Development Learning Module, In'am learned creative ways to increase her business's profit. The process of fattening and selling calves takes approximately eight months, resulting in profit generation every eight months. After the training, In'am purchased cows in order to make milk and cheese and generate a more consistent profit stream. She also learned to strategically pick a market and customer base where there is minimal competition. Ina'am was then able to expand her customer base. Now not only does she have customers in Jamaa'en, she also has a market in Nablus and its surrounding villages. Her customers constantly show their satisfaction of Ina'am's products and continue to order dairy products on a regular basis.

In'am's business is her primary focus in life. She believes in taking risks, loves the action her business brings to her life, and is fully confident that if and when she takes risks, she will succeed. In'am started her business three years ago with only three calves, but she now owns eight cows and three calves. In the future, In'am hopes to further expand her business by buying additional calves and cows which will enable her to increase her productivity. She hopes her products will become well-known and sold in every supermarket in Palestine. In'am's work is culturally categorised as man's work and she could not be more proud to break some of the gender inequality perceptions and realities in her village."[46]

A Practical Toolkit For Change

For Each Other: Actions

Part 13

The Collection of Toolkit Actions

There are things which, as women, we can all do to empower each other. Here are some key ideas, suggestions and actions which we can individually and collectively take, if we wish, to build a happier world.

I cannot and do not take credit for this toolkit. It is the result of the conversations I have had with hundreds of women worldwide who can visualise a gender equal future through all of us working together. The insights and actions come from women who call the following countries home:

United Kingdom
United States
Canada
Mexico
Australia
Germany
Iceland
Belgium
France
Spain
Portugal
United Arab Emirates
Saudi Arabia
Kuwait
Qatar
Oman
Jordan
Russia
Pakistan

This toolkit is a truly collaborative effort and call for united action. Please take what you can, do what you can and also feel enabled to add to it. Our feminist struggles continue to evolve, as must we.

Think and take action to unite

Feminist activists in both Iceland and Kuwait have demonstrated that women need a cause to unite around that captures universal attention. Uniting behind a single cause ensures that gender equality is improved through the very act of unification. What that cause is, matters less than the traction gained as an output of widespread unity.

Think. What could be the cause or trigger that women in your community or country can unite around? Identify what this might be and prepare to take advantage of the moment when it arises. Preparation needs to be in place to take action in a timely and effective way.

Women empowering women is a change that is already taking place with feminist fervour across the world. It is also a change which can accelerate faster than we ever thought possible if every member of womankind joins in with the numerous calls for unification.

There are many ways in which to be a feminist and support the end of gender inequality. Whether it is leading or following, action in some degree is necessary from all of womankind. Feminism has many guises. As long as we recognise this and support each other we have hope for an ever happier future.

Don the abaya. Ditch the abaya. Rock a bikini. Rip up a bikini. Feminism can take us in many different directions but each direction leads to the goal of gender equality. The best thing you can do is to be your own kind of feminist and speak up about why and how.

Don't just tolerate differences; value them. Feminists lead change best when they are themselves.

Foster the courage to speak out

Having the courage to speak out and share your thoughts is an important part of being included. It quite literally doesn't pay to stay quiet in meetings when you have an idea. All women should have the self belief to put themselves and their thoughts forward in order to inspire others. As women, the first thing that we can do is to speak out ourselves, and the next thing that we can do is give other women the self belief to speak up too. Either through direct encouragement or by being a good role model.

The other important aspect of speaking out is to acknowledge good ideas made by other women. Too often in meetings I have witnessed a woman share an idea which nobody appears to hear with any enthusiasm. Minutes later a man can echo the same point without acknowledging that it is an echo and gain all of the credit and exclamations of praise. When you witness this happen, speak up for your fellow woman.

"It's great that <he> echoed <her> idea and that there is so much enthusiasm around the table. Well done <her name>. A point well made and well received."

You don't have to be a loud mouth. And you don't have to give credit to anyone for what you believe to be a poor idea or approach. But you do have to cut through when it matters. Speak out in solidarity when it is needed and help other women to stand tall.

Champion relatable and unrelatable women

Many would-be female entrepreneurs have shared that seeing and hearing about a relatable role model would encourage them to start their own businesses. Talk about your story when you do something amazing (no cringing we all do amazing things) and champion other women who have great stories to tell too. Helping women to develop a greater sense of self belief is key to ensuring the next generation of female business and political leaders rise up.

There are also women who we may feel are seemingly unrelatable whose stories can inspire more women. Tell these stories too. Our gender unites us and by hearing stories from cultures and geographies totally different to ours we can often learn more than we ever thought possible. For example, an immigrant living in Kuwait may seem unrelatable to women living outside of the Middle East who have not heard of the country, but will likely not seem unrelatable to women who are Arabic or have an Arabic heritage. It can be easy to misunderstand what people are and aren't able to relate to.

For example, recently I went to a British bank to exchange my Kuwaiti Dinars for British Pounds. It was the same bank I had purchased the dinars from. The cashier (and her supervisor) both said that there was no way that they could have issued the dinars in the first place as they hadn't even heard of the country. Of course, producing my initial exchange receipt sorted the confusion which came from presenting a currency which the bank's team were not used to. Some people are great at being able to imagine themselves in different situations, but many aren't.   Therefore, it's worth remembering that relatable women and relatable environments will have a more profound impact when delivering an empowerment message.

If you are a leader, then another empowering thing you can do is to look out for the women who need training or coaching on how to stand out and create their own personal brand.   A few words of private coaching can go a long way in shaping someone's confidence and presence.

Understand gender challenges

Societies the world over still put pressure on the female to be the primary carer. There's often a lack of diversity training and education that really needs to start at a young age. There's still the traditional view that men are tougher and better at handling pressure and that women with family responsibilities might not be up for the top jobs. It comes down to knowing and understanding each gender's challenges. To empower women to gain senior roles it's important that young male professionals are enabled to have a conversation with their bosses about flexible working arrangements so that their partner can go back to work and they can both share the parenting. It's important that we support women to be able to say, "I want to get up to the next level and I also want to be involved in the upbringing of my child."

Women and men have different biologies. We can be different and equal if we take the time and care to think through gender specific challenges.

Everyday activism

Women need government support too. And we need more women in government itself. It's important to be vocal about the changes that we want to see and lobby the government to ensure that it takes action in achieving real women's economic, social and political empowerment. We must work hard, have the right attitude and claim our space.

For example, if you believe that period poverty is an issue, encourage your workplace or local shopping centres to provide sanitary protection in their washrooms for free. Or if you see adverts for Christmas gifts where girls are exclusively being steered towards toy vacuums and boys are exclusively being steered towards toy cars then call it out. If you see a safety sign amongst the roadworks saying, Men At Work, then raise it with the local Council.

I worked for a company which held an annual awards evening for its colleagues. Anyone who won an award was invited up on stage to collect a trophy from the Chief Executive. When a man won an award he would also be greeted with a handshake and a bottle of fizz and when a woman won an award she got a hug and kiss on the cheek as well as a bunch of flowers. I spoke to the Chief about this one day, respectfully pointing out that I thought it was sexist. Even though no harm was meant, men and women were being treated differently. I asked the Chief if he would consider kissing everyone who collected an award or shake hands with everyone instead. My everyday activism of highlighting the issue had a small effect: it made him think. The answer to my question, however, was an emphatic "No". But I did make the said Chief think. Hopefully that will instigate further thought and possible change in the future.

Provide platforms where women can learn

Women who are breaking through social, political and economic barriers can support other women by creating workgroups, coaching new leaders and providing safe platforms where they can learn from their mistakes and those of others. Paving a path to leadership by those already in senior positions is key to encouraging a new and diverse generation of employees.

There are lots of formal and informal ways in which you can do this. Such as:

- Mentoring or sponsoring someone.

- Arranging a networking group where women can meet on a regular basis.

- Matchmaking for leadership (not for love)! If you know a woman who would benefit from getting to know a friend or colleague of yours then introduce them.

- Be a cheerleader for fellow females when they do something well.

- Point out mistakes in private so that people can learn. It's hard to give not-so-positive feedback but when you really care about someone it's important. Keep in mind that some situations may require public feedback (handled sensitively of course) so that others can learn too.

- Set up an event where the women at work can get together and talk about issues. I currently work at a co-operative which did this. The President and our (one and only) female C-suite executive spoke about their personal and career journeys which had a profound effect on so many women who attended. The event caused some tension with the men as it was a women only event so it's essential to make sure that you head this off and explain why it is necessary.

- Set up a Facebook group or a Whatsapp group for women across various leadership levels to stay in touch.

- Write a blog about your feminist learning experiences — you can always use a pseudonym if you wish.

- Pass on books you've read to other women so that they can learn from them too.

Providing platforms for others to learn is easy. We can all change the world in our own way.

Look, look and look again

Women are less likely to apply for positions than males with the equal amount of knowledge, skills and experience. When shortlisting for interviews and there are no female candidates (in my experience within senior leadership in retail there often aren't) then it's important to consider whether the roles are being advertised in the right spaces, whether active approaches can be made to females with the required credentials, or even whether they have been screened out through gender bias. Some organisations are starting to use CV screening where the names are not made visible to employers to address gender bias (although that's not the only gender signal). To ensure that women are being given a fair chance, if the shortlist isn't balanced then look, look and look again.

Have the audacity to educate

Educational systems, or even the lack of the systems themselves, are often the biggest challenge to achieving gender parity. It's important for women to have role models, living examples who prove that women can lead, support change and thrive. Both at school and at home women are often expected to behave in a certain way and those biases and expectations come in to play in the workplace. For example, far fewer girls than boys go to engineering school or learn to code. The technology and scientific industries are the ones which will provide the leading jobs of tomorrow. Women need to encourage girls to join these fields because if we don't, the gender imbalance will become even more significant. We must encourage girls to have the audacity to try things out. To code. To create. To lead. To change.

Spot the men of average talent

As women we need to convince other women that we are as good as men and that we must demand equal space. Always remember, and remind other women, how many men of average talent have reached good positions.

Use this knowledge to get the gumption to go for things that you want; if you don't then the men certainly will. Women must not be too quiet or too humble; we must believe in ourselves. We are good enough and we should go for the promotions we deserve. Mixed gender groups always functions better and deliver stronger results so speak up about the achievements of gender equal groups.

Having gumption can mean many things such as:

- Want that job? Go for it. The worst that can happen is that you don't get it.
- Observed a man take credit for a co-worker's efforts? Amplify her voice — congratulate her on her idea.
- Found out that a male colleague doing the same job as you with the same experience is getting paid more? Ask why and ask for it to be rectified.
- Understand your company's gender pay gap and the actions in place to eliminate it.
- Does your company expect you to lead like a man when you want to lead like a woman? Ask why and demonstrate how you want to lead.

Instigating change is hard and can take many attempts. But that feeling when you achieve it is oh-

so-definitely worth it.   Do it for yourself and do it for
womankind.

Remember that giving birth isn't easy

The sad social reality of our current times is that women have to work harder and shine brighter than men to get noticed. Add giving birth into the mix and our working lives are a whole lot more challenging. Women must be given the flexibility in order to progress as one of the things we can't change is that it is women, and not men, who give birth. We must empower women to work from home if this supports them and we must also allow them to re-invent themselves after a break in their career if this is what they wish to do. Ultimately, the flexibility will pay off for both men and women through more gender diverse workplaces across levels of seniority.

It's also important to remember that the act of giving birth itself is excruciating, not to mention the marathon of pregnancy beforehand. Just because giving birth is commonplace does not mean it is any less painful. Dismissing or sneering at our female peers for pregnancy pain, pregnancy absences from work or pregnancy issues whatsoever means devaluing her personal experience. One of my friends even had the poor experience of being told by a midwife that her pushing during childbirth was "pathetic".

Give childbirth the respect it deserves. Ensure men are as responsible for childcare through paternity leave legislation and cultural expectations. Flexible hours for men benefit men and women; flexible hours for women benefit women and men. It is a current reality that men can become biological parents at any point in their lives but after menopause women cannot. Therefore, women pose less of an employment flight risk for parenthood reasons than men if parental responsibilities are equally shared. Put simply, men have more time to become parents and yet women are currently penalised with the maternity leave eye rolls.

Get social

To pave the way for the next generation of business leaders we need to show them that inclusion comes from the top. As leaders, we have a key role in helping females to break out and get to the next level. We need to stand up for women and provide them with new opportunities. In a world filled at the top with men it's important that we don't fall in to the merit trap as this is where bias finds its way in to the selection process. It's important that we have a clear and strong voice when it comes to gender equality.

Advocating for equality means being heard. Use your Twitter feed and Facebook posts to get active in the community about advocating for women and being a strong role model. It's also very useful to girls and women when you are able to be a guest speaker in the classroom, at conferences and at social gatherings. Choose the channels which work best for your story and then get communicating.

For example, my sister is a Doctor and recently ran a session with sixty schoolchildren (boys and girls) on what it is like to be in the medical profession. She also took along a Nurse and a Practice Manager (both female). After the session, the teacher said that the children were buzzing like they had never done before. Not only were they intrigued to find out the gory and gruesome details in being a doctor, (" Have you ever chopped off the wrong leg (referring to amputations)?", "What's the grossest thing you've ever done?", "Is my granny in 'eaven?") but it was also good for them to hear from women talking about the roles which they do and why they chose them. One particularly inquisitive child asked, "Why do you each do what you do?"

You could get social by chatting with people face to face or do it on social media.   Twitter is great for sharing news and short, sharp bursts of wisdom. Facebook is great for longer posts and Instagram for images.   If you're doing something feminist that will inspire others to take action, please post it on at least one network.

Take a chance

There are examples of women in senior leadership positions who have been fortunate in that someone has taken a chance on them. Women can often feel that they are not ready for a role when in fact they are; or they may not be ready for a job but would get there quickly with the right support. When you spot someone who you believe could make it but isn't quite ready, take a chance on them. Give them the support and mentoring they need to become the next senior female leader in your organisation. The impact will be felt for generations to come as she will undoubtedly do the same for someone else. Waiting for "the right time" has not gotten women anywhere very fast so far so it's time to take that chance on yourself and on someone else.

I've sometimes appointed people to roles (males and females) and it sadly hasn't worked out for them. But there are many other times when it has worked out amazingly well. You won't always get it right, but it's worth the mistakes for the times when you see someone flourish in a job which they wouldn't have been appointed to if you hadn't taken a chance on them.

Hold to account

Gender parity needs to be kept firmly on the agenda. We must encourage our own leaders to keep discussing it and measuring it. Proper commitment is needed from Chief Executives and senior leadership teams to keep gender on the agenda. At the very least, we should set ourselves and others within our teams the challenge to clearly demonstrate what we have actively done to support women in the workplace. Challenging, recording, monitoring, measuring and communicating will create the initial ripple of actions needed for enticing greater change.

I once suggested in a senior leadership team meeting at a past employer that we needed to actively do more to eradicate the organisation's culture of sexism and racism. Everyone agreed that it needed to be done, "But not now — we just don't have the time," was the general consensus. It would have been easy to stop lobbying for change by telling myself that at least I had tried. But change doesn't happen that way and the right thing to do is to hold to account and engage further. And that's exactly what I did. Getting buy in for issues which many people are complacent about is difficult.

All I know is that the result will be worth it .... in the end.

Disband the Man Club

Encouraging women to take power through their authenticity will only work if the sexist boys club in organisations is disbanded. Women need to make sure not to tolerate this club. Self-perpetuating, non-inclusive behaviour needs to be stamped out. Call out the issues with golfing days; do not accept sexist behaviour and actively voice your desire to be included in team events which are passed off as a "few drinks with the lads".

This does not mean that every male only group or event needs to be disbanded. Men need safe private spaces to chat just as women do. The clubs which need to be challenged are those which perpetuate male informal power over females. That is, what isn't acceptable is male only activity which excludes women from mentoring or sponsorship opportunities.

I sorely regret not challenging the man who said he had nicknamed a candidate he had interviewed as "TT"; I had no idea what he meant until he explained it stood for "teeth and tits". The other men who overheard this found it funny. At the time it was shock which kept me silent. Never again will I tolerate a man speaking like that about another woman. The only way to disband the club is to get comfortable with discomfort and call out the "lads will be lads" behaviour as unacceptable. This comes with risks (for example, people often now think of me as "the woman police") but they are risks which need to be taken.

Mind your language

"She wears the trousers," and many other such exclamations just aren't helpful in the gender struggle. Statements like this may be made as an acknowledgement of strength or awe but they just serve to embed women into the structure of society as secondary to men.   It's so easy to use cliche to express ourselves that although we don't mean any gender harm through our language the result is often that we are.   Next time the word, "bitch" or "cow" comes to mind, stop and think, and then find some other form of words which is fairer to our own sex.

Unconscious sexism is not okay.

Mind their language

It's all too easy to passively wince when someone else uses disempowering language in everyday situations. Like the waiter (male or female) who passes you the menus with a friendly but condescending, "Here you go girls" even though it's obvious that you're a woman and not a girl. Like your boss (male or female) who exclaims, "That's my girl" when you slam dunk a presentation. Like your male colleagues who roll their eyes and display negative body language when a new maternity leave is announced. Like the manager who says that something has gone "tits up" in a meeting.

If you act like you don't mind by allowing sexist language and sexist body language to pass by without comment or challenge, then this language will continue and in time becomes even more normalised.

When you mind, make sure people know.

Positive discrimination can have a positive place

We established in the body of this book that men have been the recipients of positive discrimination for all of their lives to some degree or another, purely because of institutionalised societal norms.

If in your sphere of life you believe that positive discrimination is the only way you can level the gender inequalities which exist, then don't shy away from it. You will be enabling equal opportunities which in deeply entrenched gender unequal workplaces can often only be tackled through numbers and quotas. For example, if there are no, or not enough, female colleagues within a certain role within your company, and despite training and action plans diversity is not forthcoming, then gender quotas may well be the action you need to take in order to enforce change. At least until gender power change is properly established.

Gender quotas on corporate boards have been used well in The Netherlands and Germany to create lasting change. No-one likes to think that they were recruited as a token gesture and quotas certainly don't condone tokens either. They just force people to look harder when they are not looking hard enough themselves.

Encouraging women to infantilise men has got to stop

In order to help themselves as well as other women, we must stop infantilising men. Is there really a good reason why women are trying to do it all and carrying the mental load? Saying, "It's just quicker when I do it" or "he doesn't do it quite the way I would" does not cut it. Women have lost all sight of their empowerment perspective when they say it's easier if they do everything themselves. Really? Easier for who exactly? Is there really such a wrong way of loading up the dishwasher or putting away the supermarket shop? And what makes women better at the school run?

Women have to stop treating men like infants or men have to stop pretending that they can't do things and pandering to infantilisation. As part of my research I met a woman who confessed that after she returned to work post maternity leave, she would dash home at lunchtimes when it was her husband's turn to be on baby duty as, "He just can't change the nappy poor thing no matter how hard he tries." Instead of taking a hard earned refreshment break she dashed home in the car to swap a dirty nappy for a clean one to last until she got home again.   Her husband was more than happy to let her do this.

There is an advert on air in the UK this year which shows a married male and female couple and their baby. The mum goes out to work and programs their intelligent home speaker to give her husband timely reminders to help him out with his baby care duties. The speaker reminds the husband that a playdate has been arranged for the afternoon, where various food stuffs are kept and finally, that the husband is "doing a great job" and is loved by his wife. The advert is for the speaker and normalises the sphere of the home and bringing up children as that of the mother, with the husband stepping in and "doing a great job" as if it was never his duty in the first place. The advert is a disappointment to watch and I am left wondering why and how somebody very senior would have signed off the advert as suitable to air.

Equality education must start in school and remain on the agenda in all workplaces

Education has been key to acceleration of gender equality in Iceland and Kuwait. It is important in primary education, secondary education, tertiary education and in the workplace. Understanding the evolving challenges of gender never stops. Even when we reach equality we need to continue education at all levels to maintain a gender equilibrium.

I was lucky enough to be taught Religious Education at school and as a result I am fluent with the beliefs and practices of all of the major faiths. This means that I can interact with people respectfully and do my job serving local communities much better than I would have been able to otherwise. Many people haven't been lucky enough to receive this education and it can seriously impact how they make sense of the world. For example, one day a customer complaint came in to my department at a retailer I worked for from someone who said that they hated my company's Easter campaign because it did not mention Jesus Christ anywhere. Most of my team thought that this was unfair criticism as a lot of people celebrate Easter as a festival and not a religious event. I reasoned that the team had a valid point, but so did the customer, as Easter was a Christian festival and centred on the resurrection of Christ. "Next you'll be telling me you don't know who Mary Magdalene is," I said in exasperation to my team. "Of course I know" piped up one of the team, "She was in last year's TV series of the 'Bake Off' ". When I had been referring to a woman of historical Christian significance, my colleague thought I was talking about a television show where people bake cakes. Understanding each other's viewpoints has never been so important as it is now.

Although my example above centres on race, it can also be applied to gender.

Education could be a lesson in a classroom at school or a meeting room at work. I recently attended a class on Movember, which was about being extra aware of male cancers during the month of November as part of a national campaign. There are similar campaigns for female cancers, such as Cysters and Breast Cancer Awareness Month.

Being made aware of inequalities means that we are more likely to become citizens who take responsibility for gender equality and other justices.

Sexual misdemeanours are never ever okay

When you spot it, experience it or witness it then you must speak out.   Sexual harassment can be used against men and women, but it is women who are faced with it significantly more often than men.   Every study ever undertaken on the topic will endorse this.

Although we know that these misdemeanours are evil it doesn't make it any easier to call them out. However, calling them out is what we must do each and every time.   It is never easy but we owe it to ourselves, our gender and humankind as a whole to make sure that we do.   It is only through acknowledging evil behaviour as unacceptable that we will make lasting change in society.   The #MeToo and #TimeIsNow campaigns specifically engaged women in calling out misogynistic behaviour.   They achieved global reach and impact.   But it doesn't stop there.

Sexual misdemeanours happen so frequently that they can often be laughed off, ignored or even worse they can oftentimes be endorsed when ignored.   It has taken me two decades to become comfortable with having uncomfortable conversations about harassment.   In calling it out I have been able to support both men and women who I have seen being victimised and doing so made it more difficult for other men to consider repeating these evils.   For example, there was a male senior manager at work once who had an obsession with lusting after women's feet.   So much so that one of my female colleagues said that she was going to come to work wearing a pair of big hairy slippers which said, "Hello" on one foot and the manager's name on the other.   The man concerned was very senior so everyone knew who he was and sadly also about his fetish, yet no-one did anything about it except laugh at his foot lusting addiction between themselves.   His behaviour made tens of women feel uncomfortable, especially about meeting him on a one to one basis.   One day I spotted him so enamoured with a colleague's feet in her peep toe shoes that he didn't hear a word that was said during our stand up huddle meeting.   He just stared and stared as if he was watching a microwave meal being cooked; waiting for the ping when he could devour it. I knew it was wrong and I could see my female colleague shifting about from foot to foot whilst everyone giggled.   That day, I reported it to my boss (the manager's peer) who took it very seriously and dealt with it appropriately.   When I look back on the incident now I wonder why several hundred of my colleagues in head office laughed about the misdemeanours and didn't do anything to stop it.   It took me about a year to come forward but it will never take me that long again.

Even today, in 2019, in one of the most developed countries in the world, I have witnessed senior leaders in a number of companies laughing at their colleagues' sexual intimidations and fetishes rather than challenging them.   The more senior the person, the harder it is to put a spotlight on it for fear of career fallout and social stigma as a man hater.   If I can give any words of encouragement to the sisterhood it would be this: you can do this.   I have spotlighted and raised the alarm about a number of male senior managers across a number of organisations.   All have been more senior than me.   I cannot say that the revelations have always been welcomed. People will often squirm and secretly despise you for raising difficult issues. However, I can confidently assert that every time I have been taken seriously and every time at least one of my female colleagues has felt the benefit of my challenge. This may not always be the case but my feelings of female solidarity are stronger than my personal fears now.

Believe me.

It feels really difficult.

It is really difficult.

But you've got this.

Notice and call out gendered ruthlessness

When you, or women around you, are confronted with challenge and criticism consider whether this is fair challenge or whether it is gendered ruthlessness. For example, the media have a tendency to use more demeaning and even demonising language when it comes to female ministers compared to male ministers.

A scan of the comments on a range of blogs also shows that public opinion is also often more ruthless towards women, both by women against women and by men against women. It is sad how far people have actually gone when writing derogatory comments online about female Members of Parliament in particular.

Here are some tweets which appeared about female Members of Parliament during the Brexit Referendum in the UK:

"Bitch. What does that cunt know? She's just good for a fuck."

"She's just a bloody idiot. What does she know about politics?"

"She hasn't got any kids. How can she give a fuck about our future without any sprogs of her own."

Gendered hostility in the UK is commonplace. Take the media harassment against Diane Abbott, MP in 2017, when all she was doing was fighting with determination for important issues. She was hounded by the press for getting her numbers wrong (a slip of the tongue which many male politicians have also experienced but not been hounded for). She stuttered with nerves at times and was penalised for being a woman, black and overweight. It was so bad that Diane actually had to take time off work to repair her health.

Take also the case of Prime Minister Theresa May; hounded by the press for delivering a poor speech because of a cough she struggled to control and a man who ran up on stage to hand her a P45 (a document which signals the end of a given employment). She could neither control her cough nor the man who sabotaged her speech with the aforementioned document, yet she was hounded because of these two things. At the Conservative Party Conference in 2018, Theresa May was congratulated by almost every newspaper in the queendom for not coughing. The content of her speech and her strategy for Brexit came second place. Point made.

Feed the world, including all of the women

Female discrimination is a serious issue which even affects the amount of food we eat or how often women and girls feel hunger pains.   Think hard about the issue of food as it lies at the heart of solving many empowerment issues.   A bowl of porridge a day can mean the difference between no education and a full time school education.   We all need a fair amount of food and nutrition to fuel our day.

Take part in collective action … with heart

Collective female action is crucial for lasting change, be this formally or informally. The Women's Day Off in Iceland evidences how powerful collective activism can be. Action can also take place across borders such as the worldwide march for women the day after Donald Trump's inauguration. The potential for collective activism, and the ensuing results, are well worth investing in both socially and politically. It was the lack of gumption for collective action on International Women's Day in my own city of Birmingham that lead me to realise why women are treated unequally. Collectively we need to make a stand for equality.

Leaving the hard work to a few individuals will not reap the results which the world needs. Please remember that just turning up because it's the right thing to do is not enough; you need to take part with your whole heart.

Hear From Helen Pankhurst

Helen introduces herself as Chancellor of the University of Suffolk, Senior Adviser at CARE International, women's rights activist and writer. She is the grand daughter of suffragette Sylvia Pankhurst and great grand daughter of Emmeline Pankhurst. Her latest book called Deeds Not Words is centred on female empowerment through the testimony of women.

She feels privileged to have had some unique and interesting experiences as a women's rights activist; from standing alongside Meryl Streep for the film Suffragette, to being involved in the opening ceremony of the latest Olympic Games. However, she asserts that her most memorable discussions have happened when she has been out "socialising my book". By this, Helen means taking her book on tour so to speak, and chatting to women, social groups, academics, booksellers, students and more about the importance of women's empowerment and her findings. Deeds Not Words focusses on the testimony of women in the United Kingdom whilst acknowledging that the UK has a vast tapestry of international influence with regards to women's issues.

I met Helen whilst she was socialising her book and she explained that although Female Genital Mutilation is a ghastly issue, it is all too easy for Brits to look outwards and place the guilt for women's disempowerment on other countries for violence against women. The UK, where so much emphasis is placed on how women look, also has its problems with issues against women. Although FGM cannot, and should not ever be compared with botox, Helen maintains that in the UK we are seeing increasing numbers of women hurting themselves by undergoing cosmetic surgery in order to change how they are physically perceived.

"In many ways we are going backwards," she says. "Cutting ourselves as women with cosmetic surgery; and social media being a place where the physical appearance of women is constantly scrutinised."

FGM in Ethiopia is the result of a cultural legacy which works against women. In much the same way that the significance of the physical appearance of women is a negative cultural legacy in Britain.

Helen grew up in Ethiopia, where she still lives for six months a year, working as a senior adviser to charity CARE International. She said that it was her upbringing in Addis Ababa, the exposure to so many different cultural norms, as well as the responsibility of the Pankhurst name, that lead her to become such a prolific women's rights activist. Seeing and experiencing two different cultures became formative in her work on class and gender. *"I would watch women doing the gruelling task of carrying water and sticks on a daily basis. This was quite literally back breaking work and yet the women were still portrayed as weak by the men."*

"If you profess to be a feminist," continues Helen, "then you are not only a believer in equality, you are required to contribute to changing inequality. My time

in Kenya taught me that there are many strands of power, with the individual at the centre of that power. An individual can have an axis of race, of gender, of religion, of class, of wealth, of nationality and so on. To make change happen there are three aspects which need to work together:

> *(1) Issues of agency (the individual)*
> *(2) Legal change*
> *(3) Social norms and values*

An individual must call out an injustice and make the decision that the injustice in question needs to change. The individual must be prepared to be the agency for that change. This calling out can then be the instigator of legal change by forcing correction of injustice or social change."

To bring this to life Helen shared the example of a receptionist at a leading corporate finance company who was sent home from work for refusing to wear high heels. The receptionist stood firm in her flats and decided to be the agent of change by launching a petition calling for the law to be changed so that companies could no longer force women to wear high heels to work.

The story gained a lot of media attention and got people talking about the issue, as well as gaining more than 152,400 signatures on an online petition and triggering a debate in Parliament. Sadly, the UK Government rejected calls to outlaw company bosses from forcing female employees to wear high heels at work and concluded that laws were already in place which were adequate to deal with discrimination on gender grounds. However, the Government has now called on all employers with dress codes to review them for gender parity.

"Women are too often judged for what they look like" says Helen, *"whilst men are judged for what they say and do"*. The example of the receptionist and her flat shoes shows that women's physical appearance carries too much significance and is reinforced in British society even today.

"In trying to address equality in society, it seems that numerical equality has become popular — such as the gender pay gap, the number of women on boards, the number of women working in engineering and so on. But feelings need to be considered with prevalence too. We need to be understanding of differences between men and women where and when they exist. Our political system has to look at the round and at the moment it doesn't."

When asked how women can empower women Helen is clear on what needs to be done:

"The narrative of sacrifice needs to be kept alive in the discourse of families. We all need to engage fully and ensure we use our right to vote as well as encouraging other women to vote. Tell your relatives about the sacrifices previous generations made on their behalf to gain the vote in order that they see their responsibility to be politically active. It's true that we do need some female only spaces so that we can envision a fair and free future. Then we need to ensure that men are part of the empowerment solution too. Issues such as violence against women

do need some safe and secure women only spaces to be effective. Then we all need to shift the needle a little bit to be individual agents of a bigger collective change.

Let's not get complacent; we are far from the last mile. My plea to women everywhere is to not take your eye off the ball. The most important thing that we can do is to champion the cause of others."

Conclusion

Part 14

Each Other

In writing this book I wanted to explore best practices outside of the United Kingdom, to bring back and offer as a suite of tools for women to empower women in the, yet to be achieved quest, for a gender equal world. I have discovered one universal truth across all of the countries which I visited.

That truth is:

We do not need miracles to change the world; we only need each other.

End Notes

Part 15

Post Script: My Wish for our World

Women empowering women is a significant and challenging change which we collectively need to make. But in writing this book, and in seeing so many global humanitarian tragedies unfold over the last few years, I am also keenly aware that the exploration and toolkit contained here is for those lucky enough to be in a position of privilege: for those who have a place to call home; who have employment; who have family and who are able to pick up books or newspapers and read about the world.

The most disempowered women are those who are fleeing political violence, living through famine, subjected to slavery or at the receiving end of extreme physical oppression. Oftentimes these issues are experienced all at once. There are millions of women worldwide for whom life offers more pain than most of us could even begin to imagine.

I think of the refugees who have perilously made their way in to the UK against all odds. Some are women, but the majority are men. Even in situations of extreme danger, it is the men who have more opportunity to flee, to hide and to survive due to the additional safety which their gender and biology carries. It is extremely difficult for the men, but near impossible for the women, given the additional setbacks and sexual violence which they face. It hurts me and haunts me that it is commonplace rhetoric to think of any human beings who are displaced and looking for new places to call home as "illegal".

I often wonder what would happen if the UK were to be submerged under water through a series of storms or destroyed by unprecedented earthquakes. Given the consequences of global warming, at some point within the next few centuries, if not sooner, it is not inconceivable that the UK could most probably be completely underwater. I wonder whether we will then expect the walls we have built around our borders to come down and whether we will see ourselves as "illegal" when searching for new homes.

Sadly, it is also commonplace to ignore issues faced by others and placate our consciences by believing that they are somebody else's problem. Putting loose change in charity shakers and focussing on your own life in your own community is good, but it is just not good enough.

Hate is dangerous but so is complacency.

Owning a heart and a brain comes with the responsibility to know that everything we do or don't do has an impact on someone else. Being silent, unaware or inactive has devastating consequences for the people who need our human kindness. In recent years within the UK there has been a trend to focus on giving and helping locally. This is all well and good, but as a country we have created and contributed to economic and social issues worldwide and therefore we also have a duty to effect positive and lasting change on both a local and global level.

Everyone has a right to shelter, food, warmth, love and compassion. Gender, sex, race, sexuality, nationality, age, religion and health should never be a barrier to full human rights. Many of us should also remember that the wealth we call ours was borne through the actions of empire, with unjust consequences which will last for centuries yet to come. The sun has yet to set on the issues caused by colonialism and the cultural imperialism which still remains.

Those of us who are privileged enough to have even the most basic of living opportunities must remember how very lucky we are. Those of us who have no home, no food and no nationality will have more imperative issues to act on than the toolkit activities in this book: educational curriculums, workplace quotas and disbanding golf clubs will certainly not be amongst them. But I do hope that in implementing the toolkit we are building a world which will be welcoming of all women and all men; which will break down its physical borders of greed and its psychological borders of fear.

My wish for the world is that we all work together to make it a happier and welcoming place for all. That we do not dance or capitalise on the misfortune of others. That we take responsibility for looking, listening and finding out about injustices the world over. That we take accountability for our part in the collective of humankind.

It is not unrealistic that one day any one of us could be a refugee of sorts: as a result of the environment, of politics, of warfare or even just for being who we are. It is imperative that we support, champion and invest in each other. I implore you to be active in demonstrating human kindness, now and every single day, in our collective future.

That is my wish for our world.

Gender Glossary

The Beijing Declaration

The Beijing Declaration is a global commitment to achieving equality, development and peace for women worldwide. It was adopted in September 1995 at the Fourth World Conference on Women, convened by the United Nations.

Female Genital Mutilation

A description for all procedures which involve partial or total removal of the external female genitalia, or other violence or injury to the female genital organs for non-medical reasons. It is also sometimes referred to as female genital cutting or female circumcision.

Feminism

Feminism has become a contentious word which can mean many different things to many different people across many different movements, philosophies and ideologies. Ultimately, it is the thinking, actions and outcomes to establish and achieve equality of the sexes.

Gender

Gender is a social construct for the expectations, opportunities, roles, responsibilities, likes, and dislikes believed to be appropriate for the sexes. Gender expression is related to gender roles and how society uses those roles to try to enforce conformity to current gender norms.

It is related to social and cultural norms linked to biological identity and not biological identity itself. Gendering begins at birth when a child's sex is identified. A child with a penis is usually identified as a boy and a child with a vulva is usually identified as a girl. A child with both a penis and a vulva is often referred to as being intersex.

Gender is not natural; it is constructed.

Gender Dysphoria
Gender dysphoria is a condition where a person experiences discomfort or distress because there's a mismatch between their biological sex and gender identity. Biological sex is assigned at birth, depending on the appearance of the genitals. Gender identity is the gender that a person identifies with or feels themselves to be.

While biological sex and gender identity are the same for most people, this isn't the case for everyone. For example, some people may have the anatomy of a man, but identify themselves as a woman, while others may not feel they're definitively either male or female.

This mismatch between sex and gender identity can lead to distressing and uncomfortable feelings that are called gender dysphoria. Gender dysphoria is a recognised medical condition by the National Health Service in the United Kingdom and also in many parts of the world, for which treatment is sometimes appropriate. Some people with gender dysphoria have a strong and persistent desire to live according to their gender identity, rather than their biological sex. These people are sometimes called transsexual or trans people. Some trans people have treatment to make their physical appearance more consistent with their gender identity.

Gender Empowerment

Gender empowerment is the fair access to opportunities and assets for people of any gender. The opportunities and assets are linked to economic participation, educational access, political participation, social freedoms and health and wellbeing. To address unfair gender realities in society there often needs to be what can be seen as an unfair focus and enablement of dis-empowered genders. It allows people to be, do and achieve things that they were previously denied. To have access to opportunity which others genders have but that they do not.

The gender which has faced consistent discrimination across social, political and economic spheres is that of the woman. It is perhaps the only discrimination that all countries have in common and why gender empowerment is often synonymous with women's empowerment and transgender empowerment.

There is more data worldwide on gender inequality than there is on gender equality; a sad reflection of the world's current unequal landscape. For a fairer future and thus a happier world, the empowerment of girls and women to achieve gender equality with boys and men must be the focus of empowerment in all social, political and economic sectors.

The Gender Empowerment Measure (GEM) is the United Nations measure of gender equality. There are also other measures in use such as the Gender

Inequality Index (GII) and the Gender Development Index (GDI) but the GEM is the most widely used within research, everyday discussion and the media.

Gender Fluid

People who identify as gender fluid don't see themselves as having a fixed gender. They may move back and forth between gender presentations and identifications, or by mixing masculine and feminine presentations. Defining "gender-fluid" is very unique to each individual who identifies with the term. The same goes for which pronouns they prefer to use and how they might choose to present their gender on any given day or time period.

Gender Identity

Gender identity is the personal sense of one's own gender. Gender identity can correlate with identified sex at birth, or can differ from it. Historically, gender was seen and talked about as binary: people generally identified as either male or female. As societies are changing, so is the concept of gender. Gender is no longer seen as binary but as a spectrum. This is because not everyone identifies with the male or female gendered identities.

A-gender people do not identify with any gender and therefore have no gender identity. Someone who identifies as gender fluid or genderqueer typically identifies neither as male or female. They might feel differently on any given day, sometimes male and sometimes female, so that they don't really identify as either a man or as a woman. A transgender person may or may not be transsexual; a person whose sense of identity and gender does not correspond with their birth sex will generally be identified as transgender. There is a complete spectrum of gender identities and some people think that the concept of gender is even broader than a spectrum.

A spectrum assumes male at one end and female at the other with degrees of identification in between. A non spectrum means that male and female are not used as the two norms against which to measure gender by if indeed it should be measured at all. The social, philosophical, psychological, physiological and religious thinking on gender is developing faster now that it has done for decades past.

Gender Spectrum

The gender spectrum exists because not everyone identifies with the societal norms associated with the sex they were identified as at birth. If a person with a penis identifies as male and a person with a vulva identifies as female then they are referred to as cisgender. This is when a person's biological sex matches with the binary gender construct of penis owners being male and vulva owners being female. The gender spectrum is a way to understand gender identity beyond the societal binary norms. The ideology of the spectrum is that everyone fits somewhere along it. A person may move across the spectrum but they will always have a place on it.

At one end of the spectrum is maleness and at the other is femaleness with degrees of maleness and femaleness in between. Language generally doesn't allow easy discussion about non-binary gender as "he" and "she" are the only singular pronouns to describe a person albeit new pronouns are being invented and championed, but are yet to be accepted widely in to everyday lexicon.

Gender is constructed and therefore is no longer considered binary.

Intersectionality
The concept that oppression within society, such as sexism, racism, ageism and homophobia, do not and cannot act independently, but are instead interrelated and continuously shaped by one another. It starts from the premise that people have multiple, layered identities derived from social relations, history and the operation of structures of power. Intersectional analysis aims to reveal multiple identities, exposing the different types of discrimination and disadvantage that occur as a consequence of the combination of identities. It aims to address the manner in which racism, patriarchy, class oppression and other systems of discrimination create inequalities that structure the relative positions of women.

Mysogyny
The hatred of, contempt for, or prejudice against women or girls.

Patriarchy
Systemic societal structures that institutionalise male physical, social and economic power over women.

Phallology
The scientific study of the penis

Phallocentric

The cultural and social organisation of the world fostered by what is referred to as the patriarchy.

Suffragette
A woman who campaigned for the right of women to vote, especially a member of the early twentieth century British group of activists lead by Emmeline Pankhurst and Christabel Pankhurst.

Suffragist
The advocation and campaigning of women's suffrage without the use of organised violence. Millicent Fawcett is deemed to have been the leading suffragist within the UK.

United Nations Gender Inequality Index
This is an index for measurement of gender disparity that was introduced in the 2010 Human Development Report 20th anniversary edition by the United Nations Development Programme (UNDP).

The World Economic Forum
This is an International organisation for public-private cooperation. It was established in 1971 as a not-for-profit foundation and is headquartered in Geneva, Switzerland. It claims to be independent, impartial and not tied to any special interests. Moral and intellectual integrity is at the heart of everything it does.

References

Full credit to:

(1) Facts & Figures Report, UN Women, cited from October 2018 search: http://www.unwomen.org/en/what-we-do/youth/facts-and-figures

(2) International Women's Day Campaign Article, UN Women, cited from June 2018 search:

(3) International Women's Day Strike Event Article, The British Broadcasting Corporation, cited from November 2018 search

(4) 21 Facts About Gender Inequality You Need to Know Now Article, Makers, cited from search March 2018: https://www.makers.com/blog/21-facts-you-never-knew-about-international-gender-inequality

(5) The Global Gender Gap Report, 2017 Version, World Economic Forum, https://www.weforum.org/reports/the-global-gender-gap-report-2017

(6) Global Female Leaders Conference, Berlin 2018, Germany, https://www.globalfemaleleaders.com/

(7) State Street Global Advisers Report, Global Female Leaders, Berlin 2018

(8) TIME 100 Most Influential, 2013 List, http://time100.time.com/2013/04/18/time-100/slide/all/

(9) Roya Mahboob, Digital Citizen Fund, Company Website http://digitalcitizenfund.org/

(10) Shoes & Fashion Website, Zalando, http://www.zalando.com/

(11) European Space Agency, https://www.esa.int/ESA

(12) UN Trust Fund to End Violence Against Women, UN Women Organisation, http://www.unwomen.org/en/trust-funds/un-trust-fund-to-end-violence-against-women

(13) Story content approved by Valerie Dwyer, United Kingdom

(14) May Wong, Domestic Help in China Article, Solidarity Feminist Organisation, cited from November 2018 search https://solidarity-us.org/atc/133/p1394/

(15) Ashleigh Millman, Twitter Feed @ashmillman, https://twitter.com/ashmillman/status/1017051801303109632

(16) Global Property Guide Report, Global Property, Iceland Edition, cited from June 2018 search https://www.globalpropertyguide.com/Europe/Iceland

(17) Unicef Press Release on Paternity Leave, cited from search November 2018 https://www.unicef.org/press-releases/2-3-infants-live-countries-where-dads-are-not-entitled-single-day-paid-paternity

(18) World Policy Center, Report on Paid Paternity Leave, cited from search November 2018 https://www.worldpolicycenter.org/policies/is-paid-leave-available-to-mothers-and-fathers-of-infants/is-paid-leave-available-for-fathers-of-infants

(19) Statistics Iceland, cited search October 2018 https://www.statice.is

(20) The Paternity Leave Act in Iceland, cited search November 2018 https://www.researchgate.net/publication/46528219_The_Paternity_Leave_Act_in_Iceland_implications_for_gender_equality_in_the_labour_market

(21) Story content supplied and approved by Deborah Rodriguez, Mexico

(22) Artist Reference, https://www.artspace.com/artist/james_de_la_vega

(23) Icelandic Women's Rights Association, http://kvenrettindafelag.is/en/

(24) Icelandic Arctic Co-operation Network, https://arcticiceland.is/en/adhilar/jafnrettisstofa

(25) Issues of intersection are touched upon in Kabeer, Stark and Magnus' book, Global Perspectives on Gender Equality: Reversing the Gaze, 2008, Routledge Press

(26) The topic of gender in Iceland is explored in depth in Johnson's book, The Gender of Informal Politics: Russia, Iceland and Twenty-First Century Male Dominance, 2018, Palgrave Macmillan

(27) The Icelandic Phallological Museum Leaflet, issued to visitors, received on 2018 visit

(28) Photos taken by visitors at The Icelandic Phallological Museum can be seen on the organisations's website and via a Google search.

(29) The Icelandic "Women's Day Off" campaign poster for 2018 had just come back from the printers during my visit to The Women's House.

(30) Nordiskt Forum Malmö (New Action on Women's Rights), 2014, http://nf2014.org/en/

(31) United Nations Development Programme, UNDP Gender Inequality Index Report, cited search November 2018 http://hdr.undp.org/en/content/gender-inequality-index-gii

(32) Forbes 100 Most Powerful Arab Women list, October 2018, https://www.forbesmiddleeast.com/en/list/top-100-powerful-arab-businesswomen-2018/

(33) Alessandra L. Gonzalez, Islamic Feminism in Kuwait: The Politics and Paradoxes, Palgrave Macmillan, 2014

(34) Haya al-Mughni, Women in Kuwait: The Politics of Gender, Saqi Books, 2001

(35) Story content supplied and approved by Sarah Ajlouny, Jordan

(36) Guerilla Girls Talk Back Group Website, https://www.guerrillagirls.com/#open

(37) The Gulabi Gang, India, cited search October 2018 http://gulabigang.in/

(38) The Me Too Movement, https://metoomvmt.org/

(39) Story content supplied and approved by Nasira Habib, Pakistan

(40) Radhika Sanghani, Burka Bans: The Countries Where Muslim Women Can't Wear Veils, Article, cited search September 2018 https://www.telegraph.co.uk/women/life/burka-bans-the-countries-where-muslim-women-cant-wear-veils/

(41) I met Helen Pankhurst at the Deeds Not Words Event, Birmingham Literature Festival, Birmingham, UK, https://www.birminghamliteraturefestival.org/Events/Deeds-Not-Words-by-Helen-Pankhurst.

(42) World Hunger Education Service, Hunger Notes document, cited search June 2018, https://www.worldhunger.org/world-hunger-and-poverty-facts-and-statistics/

(43) Financial Times, Gender Pay Gap: How Women Are Short Changed in the UK, article, https://ig.ft.com/gender-pay-gap-UK/

(44) Story content written and published by Godfrey Oyekorredo, The Girls Empowerment Centre, Kenya on the GlobalGiving website, https://www.globalgiving.org/donate/30793/nyanza-initiative-for-girls-education-and-empowerment-n/ and approved for use in this book

(45) Story content written and published by Theresa Zimmer, La Casa de Panchita, Peru on the GlobalGiving website https://www.globalgiving.org/projects/give-girls-in-domestic-work-a-safe-place-in-peru/ and approved for use in this book by LCdP

(46) Story content written and published by Rawan Musameh, Tomorrow's Youth Organisation, Palestine on the GlobalGiving website https://

www.globalgiving.org/projects/tyowep/ and approved for use in this book by TYO

Appendix

Materials included for your reference:

- Global Gender Gap Index

- Global Gender Equality Rankings 2017

- United Nations Gender Equality Targets (Sustainable Development Goal 5)

- Policies to Promote Fathers' Uptake of Parental Leave

Global Gender Gap Index

There is not a single nation in the world that has a World Economic Forum gender parity score of 100%.

The Global Gender Gap Index was first introduced by the World Economic Forum in 2006 as a framework for capturing the magnitude of gender-based disparities and tracking their progress over time. This year's edition of the Report benchmarks 144 countries on their progress towards gender parity on a scale from 0 (imparity) to 1 (parity) across four thematic dimensions —

- Economic Participation and Opportunity
- Educational Attainment
- Health and Survival
- Political Empowerment

It provides country rankings that allow for effective comparisons across regions and income groups. The rankings are designed to create global awareness of the challenges posed by gender gaps and the opportunities created by reducing them. The methodology and quantitative analysis behind the rankings are intended to serve as a basis for designing effective measures for reducing gender gaps. The methodology of the Index has remained stable since its original conception in 2006, providing a basis for robust cross-country and time-series analysis.

The 2017 Report's key findings are:

- Weighted by population, in 2017, the average progress on closing the global gender gap stands at 68.0%— meaning an average gap of 32.0% remains to be closed worldwide across the four Index dimensions in order to achieve universal gender parity, compared to an average gap of 31.7% last year.

- On average, the 144 countries covered in the Report have closed 96% of the gap in health outcomes between women and men, unchanged since last year, and more than 95% of the gap in educational attainment, a slight decrease compared to last year. However, the gaps between women and men on economic participation and political empowerment remain wide: only 58% of the economic participation gap has been closed—a second consecutive year of reversed progress and the lowest value measured by the Index since 2008 —and about 23% of the political gap, unchanged since last year against a long-term trend of slow but steady improvement.

- Despite this overall mixed picture and continued stalling of progress at the global level, the situation is more nuanced at the regional and country level. Out of the 142 countries covered by the Index both this year and last year, 82 countries have increased their overall gender gap score compared to last year, while 60 have seen it decrease. By contrast, last year's Report found negative outcomes in more than half of countries surveyed. Moreover, as detailed in the Report, a number of countries and regions have crossed symbolic milestones on the path to gender parity for the first time this year.

- Although this year's edition of the Global Gender Gap Index sees no new entrants to its top 10 list, there have been notable rank changes. The top spots continue to be held by smaller Western European countries, particularly the Nordics that occupy the top three positions, with two countries from the East Asia and the Pacific region, one country from the Sub-Saharan Africa region, one country from the Latin America and the Caribbean region, and one country from the Eastern Europe and Central Asia region also represented. All but three countries in the Index top 10 have now crossed the threshold of closing more than 80% of their overall gender gap—up from five both last year and in 2015.

- At a global level, in 2017 four regions have a remaining gender gap of less than 30%—two of which are crossing this threshold for the first time this year. Western Europe records a remaining gender gap of 25%, placing it ahead of North America, with a gap of 28%, Eastern Europe and Central Asia, with a gap of 29%, and Latin America and the Caribbean, with a gap of 29.8%. The East Asia and the Pacific region ranks ahead of Sub-Saharan Africa, with a remaining gender gap of 31.7% and 32.4%, respectively, and South Asia, with a gap of 34%. The Middle East and North Africa region, for the first time this year, crosses the threshold of having a remaining gender gap of slightly less than 40%.

Global Gender Equality Rankings 2017

Countries marked with an asterisk* are referred to or used as examples within Each Other.

Country	Rank
Iceland*	1
Norway	2
Finland	3
Rwanda	4
Sweden*	5
Nicaragua	6
Slovenia	7
Ireland	8
New Zealand	9
Philippines	10
France*	11
Germany*	12
Namibia	13
Denmark*	14
United Kingdom*	15
Canada*	16
Bolivia	17

Bulgaria	18
South Africa	19
Latvia	20
Switzerland*	21
Burundi	22
Barbados	23
Spain*	24
Cuba	25
Belarus	26
Bahamas	27
Lithuania	28
Mozambique	29
Moldova	30
Belgium	31
Netherlands	32
Portugal*	33
Argentina	34
Australia	35
Colombia	36
Estonia	37
Albania	38

Poland*	39
Serbia	40
Costa Rica	41
Ecuador	42
Panama	43
Israel	44
Uganda	45
Botswana	46
Bangladesh*	47
Peru*	48
United States*	49
Zimbabwe	50
Jamaica	51
Kazakhstan*	52
Mongolia*	53
Croatia	54
Honduras	55
Uruguay	56
Austria	57
Romania	58
Luxembourg	59

Venezuela	60
Ukraine	61
El Salvador	62
Chile	63
Lao PDR	64
Singapore*	65
Bosnia and Herzegovina	66
Macedonia, FYR	67
Tanzania	68
Vietnam	69
Dominican Republic	70
Russian Federation*	71
Ghana	72
Lesotho	73
Slovak Republic	74
Thailand*	75
Kenya*	76
Montenegro	77
Greece	78
Belize	79
Madagascar*	80

Mexico*	81
Italy*	82
Myanmar	83
Indonesia	84
Kyrgyz Republic	85
Suriname	86
Cameroon	87
Czech Republic	88
Cape Verde	89
Brazil	90
Senegal	91
Cyprus	92
Malta	93
Georgia	94
Tajikistan*	95
Paraguay	96
Armenia	97
Azerbaijan	98
Cambodia	99
China*	100
Malawi	101

Brunei Darussalam	102
Hungary	103
Malaysia	104
Swaziland	105
Maldives	106
Liberia	107
India*	108
Sri Lanka	109
Guatemala	110
Nepal	111
Mauritius	112
Guinea	113
Japan	114
Ethiopia	115
Benin	116
Tunisia	117
Korea, Rep.	118
Gambia, The	119
United Arab Emirates*	120
Burkina Faso	121
Nigeria	122

Angola	123
Bhutan	124
Fiji	125
Bahrain*	126
Algeria	127
Timor-Leste	128
Kuwait*	129
Qatar*	130
Turkey*	131
Mauritania	132
Cote d'Ivoire	133
Egypt*	134
Jordan*	135
Morocco*	136
Lebanon*	137
Saudi Arabia*	138
Mali	139
Iran, Islamic Rep.*	140
Chad	141
Syria*	142
Pakistan*	143

Yemen*	144

Credit: Cited from The Global Gender Gap Report 2017 by The World Economic Forum. The report can be found in its full form here:

https://www.weforum.org/reports/the-global-gender-gap-report-2017

Asterisks* added for illustrative purposes by the author.

United Nations Gender Equality Targets
(Sustainable Development Goal 5)

Gender equality is not only a fundamental human right, but a necessary foundation for a peaceful, prosperous and sustainable world. Unfortunately, at the current time, 1 in 5 women and girls between the ages of 15-49 have reported experiencing physical or sexual violence by an intimate partner within a 12-month period and 49 countries currently have no laws protecting women from domestic violence. Progress is occurring regarding harmful practices such as child marriage and FGM (Female Genital Mutilation), which has declined by 30% in the past decade, but there is still much work to be done to complete eliminate such practices.

Providing women and girls with equal access to education, health care, decent work, and representation in political and economic decision-making processes will fuel sustainable economies and benefit societies and humanity at large. Implementing new legal frameworks regarding female equality in the workplace and the eradication of harmful practices targeted at women is crucial to ending the gender-based discrimination prevalent in many countries around the world.

- End all forms of discrimination against all women and girls everywhere

- Eliminate all forms of violence against all women and girls in the public and private spheres, including trafficking and sexual and other types of exploitation

- Eliminate all harmful practices, such as child, early and forced marriage and female genital mutilation

- Recognise and value unpaid care and domestic work through the provision of public services, infrastructure and social protection policies and the promotion of shared responsibility within the household and the family as nationally appropriate

- Ensure women's full and effective participation and equal opportunities for leadership at all levels of decision making in political, economic and public life

- Ensure universal access to sexual and reproductive health and reproductive rights as agreed in accordance with the Programme of Action of the International Conference on Population and Development and the Beijing Platform for Action and the outcome documents of their review conferences

- Undertake reforms to give women equal rights to economic resources, as well as access to ownership and control over land and other forms of property, financial services, inheritance and natural resources, in accordance with national laws

- Enhance the use of enabling technology, in particular information and communications technology, to promote the empowerment of women

- Adopt and strengthen sound policies and enforceable legislation for the promotion of gender equality and the empowerment of all women and girls at all levels

Credit: Cited directly from the United Nations Sustainable Development Goals. The full document can be found here: https://www.un.org/sustainabledevelopment/gender-equality/

Policies to Promote Fathers' Uptake of Parental Leave

Economy	Examples
Austria	Parents each receive an additional bonus payment if they share their leave equally or at least 60:40
France	Parents receive higher payments if they both take the same leave
Italy	Parents receive an additional month of leave if the father takes at least 3 of the initial 10 months
Germany	Parents receive pay for an additional 2 months of paid leave if they share the initial 12 months
Sweden	90 of the 480 days parental leave are reserved for each parent

World Bank Group. 2018. Women, Business and the Law 2018. Washington, DC: World Bank. License: Creative Commons Attribution CC BY 3.0 IGO

Further Reading

United Nations Sustainable Development Goals
sustainabledevelopment.un.org

The Winston Churchill Memorial Trust
wcmt.org.uk

The Rank Foundation
rankfoundation.com

GlobalGiving UK
globalgiving.org

Shoes by Shaherazad
shaherazad.com

Start Empowering Today

If you were inspired by the stories of Laurine, Sheyla and In'am then you may wish to help other girls and women who are currently living in poverty. A simple way to consciously help is by making a donation directly to a project which interests you via www.globalgiving.com.

You could also treat yourself to a shiny new pair of shoes or shoellery from www.shaherazad.com. Be happy in the knowledge that new shoes for you, means a girl living in poverty is gaining funds for an education so that she can achieve independence through meaningful long-term employment.

As a thank you gift from me to you for reading this book, please accept twenty per cent off any full price treat on the Shoes by Shaherazad website. Just enter this code on checking out to redeem:*

EachOther20

Good luck with empowering yourself and each other.

In Solidarity,

Shaherazad

Shoe.E.O.
Shoes by Shaherazad

* The **EachOther20** offer may be closed by the author at her discretion at any time.

Acknowledgements

Huge thanks go to every woman and every girl who has shared their personal experiences and statistical information for this book. Particular thanks go to: Deborah Rodriguez, Hanifa Shah, Farah Alali, Brynhildur Heiðar and Nasira Habib. You not only provided heartfelt stories and thought provoking insights but have also spent valuable time to cheerlead me on. You have all truly empowered me.

Thank you also to:

- **The Winston Churchill Memorial Trust** and **The Rank Foundation** for funding my visits to Germany, Iceland and Kuwait and for providing robust support through their Fellowship networks.

- **The Department for International Trade** (United Kingdom) for providing me with an amount of financial support to visit several international markets to develop Shoes by Shaherazad.

- **The United Nations Trust Fund to End Violence Against Women** for inviting me to The Tower of London for the launch of their empowering campaign.

- **KTV2 (Kuwait Television Channel 2)** for hosting me on their programme, Tea Time Kuwait to talk about women's empowerment.

- **GlobalGiving UK** for their support in providing the infrastructure to get funding to the women and girls who need it most. In helping me to find empowering projects you have enabled me to help many little girls who are in need of extra love and care.

- Every organisation I visited during my research trips for providing me with clear insights, challenging discussions and ideas for further empowering exploration.

- **Central England Co-operative** for being a forward thinking organisation by allowing me to take a sabbatical so that I could complete my Churchill Fellowship, write my book and empower women's lives through building my footwear brand.

- My team and customers at **Shoes by Shaherazad**. I am so very thankful that there are people like you in the world who play an active part in alleviating the suffering of others through your conscious ethical decision making.

- My colleagues and friends who have spent hours reading, editing and proofing the book. Especially Suna, Irrum, May, Kay, Carole, David and David.

Special hugs and my heartfelt appreciation to:

- Kara for being prepared to accompany me on the wildest and strangest adventures and the ever-present generosity of your time.

- David for looking out for me as a true kindred spirit. I will always appreciate your encouragement for me to cultivate my innate strangeness. Thank you so very much.

- My female-powered-family who have always been and continue to be my cheerleaders; enabling me to live, work, travel, read, write, think, dream and do. Thank you Zurren, Mehreen, Irrum and Suna.

The Author

Shaherazad Umbreen lives and works in Birmingham, England. Her life goals are the empowerment of women and the alleviation of poverty. She is Head of Customer & Marketing at The Co-operative (**Central England Co-operative**), Shoe.E.O of her own purposeful company called **Shoes by Shaherazad**, and Patron at **Raising Futures: Kenya**. She has won a number of awards for her achievements in business, enterprise, design and international trade.

You can **contact Shaherazad**:
- On Twitter @shazumbreen
- Via email through shaherazad.com
- Or in person when she is working on her latest project from The Library of Birmingham

You can also **join her mailing list** by subscribing at: shaherazad.com when you search for "Get the Latest"

Her shoe empowerment **blog** can be followed and contributed to at:
shaherazad.com/blogs/news

Further contributions to the toolkit are very welcome.

Printed in Poland
by Amazon Fulfillment
Poland Sp. z o.o., Wrocław